Lua 5.1 Reference Manual

Lua 5.1 Reference Manual

Roberto Ierusalimschy

PUC-Rio

Luiz Henrique de Figueiredo

IMPA

Waldemar Celes

PUC-Rio

Lua.org

Rio de Janeiro, Brazil

Lua 5.1 Reference Manual

by Roberto Ierusalimschy, Luiz Henrique de Figueiredo, and Waldemar Celes.

ISBN 85-903798-3-3

The authors can be contacted at `team@lua.org`.

Book cover and illustrations by Dimaquina. Lua logo design by Alexandre Nako. Typesetting by the authors using LaTeX.

Contents

1 Introduction

Lua is an extension programming language designed to support general procedural programming with data description facilities. It also offers good support for object-oriented programming, functional programming, and data-driven programming. Lua is intended to be used as a powerful, light-weight scripting language for any program that needs one. Lua is implemented as a library, written in *clean* C (that is, in the common subset of ANSI C and C++).

Being an extension language, Lua has no notion of a "main" program: it only works *embedded* in a host client, called the *embedding program* or simply the *host*. This host program can invoke functions to execute a piece of Lua code, can write and read Lua variables, and can register C functions to be called by Lua code. Through the use of C functions, Lua can be augmented to cope with a wide range of different domains, thus creating customized programming languages sharing a syntactical framework. The Lua distribution includes a sample host program called lua, which uses the Lua library to offer a complete, stand-alone Lua interpreter.

Lua is free software, and is provided as usual with no guarantees, as stated in its license. The implementation described in this manual is available at Lua's official web site, www.lua.org.

Like any other reference manual, this document is dry in places. For a discussion of the decisions behind the design of Lua, see the technical papers available at Lua's web site. For a detailed introduction to programming in Lua, see Roberto's book, *Programming in Lua (Second Edition)*.

2   The Language

This section describes the lexis, the syntax, and the semantics of Lua. In other words, this section describes which tokens are valid, how they can be combined, and what their combinations mean.

The language constructs will be explained using the usual extended BNF notation, in which {*a*} means 0 or more *a*'s, and [*a*] means an optional *a*. Non-terminals are shown like *non-terminal*, keywords are shown like **kword**, and other terminal symbols are shown like '='. The complete syntax of Lua can be found at the end of this manual.

2.1   Lexical Conventions

Names (also called *identifiers*) in Lua can be any string of letters, digits, and underscores, not beginning with a digit. This coincides with the definition of names in most languages. (The definition of letter depends on the current locale: any character considered alphabetic by the current locale can be used in an identifier.) Identifiers are used to name variables and table fields.

The following *keywords* are reserved and cannot be used as names:

and	break	do	else	elseif
end	false	for	function	if
in	local	nil	not	or
repeat	return	then	true	until	while

Lua is a case-sensitive language: and is a reserved word, but And and AND are two different, valid names. As a convention, names starting with an underscore followed by uppercase letters (such as _VERSION) are reserved for internal global variables used by Lua.

The following strings denote other tokens:

```
+       -       *       /       %       ^       #
==      ~=      <=      >=      <       >       =
(       )       {       }       [       ]
;       :       ,       .       ..      ...
```

Literal strings can be delimited by matching single or double quotes, and can contain the following C-like escape sequences: '\a' (bell), '\b' (backspace), '\f' (form feed), '\n' (newline), '\r' (carriage return), '\t' (horizontal tab), '\v' (vertical tab), '\\' (backslash), '\"' (quotation mark [double quote]), and '\'' (apostrophe [single quote]). Moreover, a backslash followed by a real newline results in a newline in the string. A character in a string may also be specified by its numerical value using the escape sequence *ddd*, where *ddd* is a sequence of up to three decimal digits. (Note that if a numerical escape is to be followed by a digit, it must be expressed using exactly three digits.) Strings in Lua may contain any 8-bit value, including embedded zeros, which can be specified as '\0'.

To put a double (single) quote, a newline, a backslash, or an embedded zero inside a literal string enclosed by double (single) quotes you must use an escape sequence. Any other character may be directly inserted into the literal. (Some control characters may cause problems for the file system, but Lua has no problem with them.)

Literal strings can also be defined using a long format enclosed by *long brackets*. We define an *opening long bracket of level n* as an opening square bracket followed by *n* equal signs followed by another opening square bracket. So, an opening long bracket of level 0 is written as [[, an opening long bracket of level 1 is written as [=[, and so on. A *closing long bracket* is defined similarly; for instance, a closing long bracket of level 4 is written as]====]. A long string starts with an opening long bracket of any level and ends at the first closing long bracket of the same level. Literals in this bracketed form may run for several lines, do not interpret any escape sequences, and ignore long brackets of any other level. They may contain anything except a closing bracket of the proper level.

For convenience, when the opening long bracket is immediately followed by a newline, the newline is not included in the string. As an example, in a system using ASCII (in which 'a' is coded as 97, newline is coded as 10, and '1' is coded as 49), the five literals below denote the same string:

```
a = 'alo\n123"'
a = "alo\n123\""
a = '\97lo\10\04923"'
a = [[alo
123"]]
a = [==[
alo
123"]==]
```

A *numerical constant* may be written with an optional decimal part and an optional decimal exponent. Lua also accepts integer hexadecimal constants, by prefixing them with 0x. Examples of valid numerical constants are

```
3    3.0    3.1416    314.16e-2    0.31416E1    0xff    0x56
```

A *comment* starts with a double hyphen (--) anywhere outside a string. If the text immediately after -- is not an opening long bracket, the comment is a *short comment*, which runs until the end of the line. Otherwise, it is a *long comment*, which runs until the corresponding closing long bracket. Long comments are frequently used to disable code temporarily.

2.2 Values and Types

Lua is a *dynamically typed language*. This means that variables do not have types; only values do. There are no type definitions in the language. All values carry their own type.

All values in Lua are *first-class values*. This means that all values can be stored in variables, passed as arguments to other functions, and returned as results.

There are eight basic types in Lua: *nil, boolean, number, string, function,*
userdata, thread, and *table*. *Nil* is the type of the value **nil**, whose main property
is to be different from any other value; it usually represents the absence of
a useful value. *Boolean* is the type of the values **false** and **true**. Both **nil**
and **false** make a condition false; any other value makes it true. *Number*
represents real (double-precision floating-point) numbers. (It is easy to build
Lua interpreters that use other internal representations for numbers, such as
single-precision float or long integers; see file luaconf.h.) *String* represents
arrays of characters. Lua is 8-bit clean: strings may contain any 8-bit character,
including embedded zeros ('\0') (see §2.1).

Lua can call (and manipulate) functions written in Lua and functions written
in C (see §2.5.8).

The type *userdata* is provided to allow arbitrary C data to be stored in Lua
variables. This type corresponds to a block of raw memory and has no pre-
defined operations in Lua, except assignment and identity test. However, by
using *metatables*, the programmer can define operations for userdata values
(see §2.8). Userdata values cannot be created or modified in Lua, only through
the C API. This guarantees the integrity of data owned by the host program.

The type *thread* represents independent threads of execution and it is used
to implement coroutines (see §2.11). Do not confuse Lua threads with operating-
system threads. Lua supports coroutines on all systems, even those that do not
support threads.

The type *table* implements associative arrays, that is, arrays that can be
indexed not only with numbers, but with any value (except **nil**). Tables can be
heterogeneous; that is, they can contain values of all types (except **nil**). Tables
are the sole data structuring mechanism in Lua; they may be used to represent
ordinary arrays, symbol tables, sets, records, graphs, trees, etc. To represent
records, Lua uses the field name as an index. The language supports this
representation by providing a.name as syntactic sugar for a["name"]. There are
several convenient ways to create tables in Lua (see §2.5.7).

Like indices, the value of a table field can be of any type (except **nil**). In
particular, because functions are first-class values, table fields may contain
functions. Thus tables may also carry *methods* (see §2.5.9).

Tables, functions, threads, and (full) userdata values are *objects*: variables
do not actually *contain* these values, only *references* to them. Assignment,
parameter passing, and function returns always manipulate references to such
values; these operations do not imply any kind of copy.

The library function type returns a string describing the type of a given
value.

2.2.1   Coercion

Lua provides automatic conversion between string and number values at run
time. Any arithmetic operation applied to a string tries to convert this string to
a number, following the usual conversion rules. Conversely, whenever a number
is used where a string is expected, the number is converted to a string, in a

reasonable format. For complete control over how numbers are converted to strings, use the `format` function from the string library (see `string.format` on page 74).

2.3 Variables

Variables are places that store values.

There are three kinds of variables in Lua: global variables, local variables, and table fields.

A single name can denote a global variable or a local variable (or a function's formal parameter, which is a particular kind of local variable):

> *var* → Name

Name denotes identifiers, as defined in §2.1.

Any variable is assumed to be global unless explicitly declared as a local (see §2.4.7). Local variables are *lexically scoped*: local variables can be freely accessed by functions defined inside their scope (see §2.6).

Before the first assignment to a variable, its value is **nil**.

Square brackets are used to index a table:

> *var* → *prefixexp* '[' *exp* ']'

The meaning of accesses to global variables and table fields can be changed via metatables. An access to an indexed variable `t[i]` is equivalent to a call `gettable_event(t,i)`. (See §2.8 for a complete description of the `gettable_event` function. This function is not defined or callable in Lua. We use it here only for explanatory purposes.)

The syntax var.Name is just syntactic sugar for var["Name"]:

> *var* → *prefixexp* '.' Name

All global variables live as fields in ordinary Lua tables, called *environment tables* or simply *environments* (see §2.9). Each function has its own reference to an environment, so that all global variables in this function will refer to this environment table. When a function is created, it inherits the environment from the function that created it. To get the environment table of a Lua function, you call `getfenv`. To replace it, you call `setfenv`. (You can only manipulate the environment of C functions through the debug library; (see §5.9).)

An access to a global variable x is equivalent to _env.x, which in turn is equivalent to

```
gettable_event(_env, "x")
```

where _env is the environment of the running function. (See §2.8 for a complete description of the `gettable_event` function. This function is not defined or callable in Lua. Similarly, the _env variable is not defined in Lua. We use them here only for explanatory purposes.)

2.4 Statements

Lua supports an almost conventional set of statements, similar to those in
Pascal or C. This set includes assignment, control structures, function calls,
and variable declarations.

2.4.1 Chunks

The unit of execution of Lua is called a *chunk*. A chunk is simply a sequence of
statements, which are executed sequentially. Each statement can be optionally
followed by a semicolon:

> *chunk*   →   {*stat* ['*;*']}

There are no empty statements and thus '*;;*' is not legal.

Lua handles a chunk as the body of an anonymous function with a variable
number of arguments (see §2.5.9). As such, chunks can define local variables,
receive arguments, and return values.

A chunk may be stored in a file or in a string inside the host program. When a
chunk is executed, first it is pre-compiled into instructions for a virtual machine,
and then the compiled code is executed by an interpreter for the virtual machine.

Chunks may also be pre-compiled into binary form; see program luac for
details. Programs in source and compiled forms are interchangeable; Lua automatically detects the file type and acts accordingly.

2.4.2 Blocks

A block is a list of statements; syntactically, a block is the same as a chunk:

> *block*   →   *chunk*

A block may be explicitly delimited to produce a single statement:

> *stat*   →   **do** *block* **end**

Explicit blocks are useful to control the scope of variable declarations. Explicit
blocks are also sometimes used to add a **return** or **break** statement in the
middle of another block (see §2.4.4).

2.4.3 Assignment

Lua allows multiple assignment. Therefore, the syntax for assignment defines
a list of variables on the left side and a list of expressions on the right side. The
elements in both lists are separated by commas:

> *stat*   →   *varlist1* '*=*' *explist1*
> *varlist1*   →   *var* {'*,*' *var*}
> *explist1*   →   *exp* {'*,*' *exp*}

Expressions are discussed in §2.5.

Before the assignment, the list of values is *adjusted* to the length of the list
of variables. If there are more values than needed, the excess values are thrown

away. If there are fewer values than needed, the list is extended with as many **nil**'s as needed. If the list of expressions ends with a function call, then all values returned by this call enter in the list of values, before the adjustment (except when the call is enclosed in parentheses; see §2.5).

The assignment statement first evaluates all its expressions and only then are the assignments performed. Thus the code

```
i = 3
i, a[i] = i+1, 20
```

sets a[3] to 20, without affecting a[4] because the i in a[i] is evaluated (to 3) before it is assigned 4. Similarly, the line

```
x, y = y, x
```

exchanges the values of x and y.

The meaning of assignments to global variables and table fields can be changed via metatables. An assignment to an indexed variable t[i]=val is equivalent to settable_event(t,i,val). (See §2.8 for a complete description of the settable_event function. This function is not defined or callable in Lua. We use it here only for explanatory purposes.)

An assignment to a global variable x=val is equivalent to the assignment _env.x=val, which in turn is equivalent to

```
settable_event(_env, "x", val)
```

where _env is the environment of the running function. (The _env variable is not defined in Lua. We use it here only for explanatory purposes.)

2.4.4 Control Structures

The control structures **if**, **while**, and **repeat** have the usual meaning and familiar syntax:

stat	→	**while** *exp* **do** *block* **end**
stat	→	**repeat** *block* **until** *exp*
stat	→	**if** *exp* **then** *block* { **elseif** *exp* **then** *block* } [**else** *block*] **end**

Lua also has a **for** statement, in two flavors (see §2.4.5).

The condition expression of a control structure may return any value. Both **false** and **nil** are considered false. All values different from **nil** and **false** are considered true (in particular, the number 0 and the empty string are also true).

In the **repeat–until** loop, the inner block does not end at the **until** keyword, but only after the condition. So, the condition can refer to local variables declared inside the loop block.

The **return** statement is used to return values from a function or a chunk (which is just a function). Functions and chunks may return more than one value, so the syntax for the **return** statement is

stat	→	**return** [*explist1*]

The **break** statement is used to terminate the execution of a **while**, **repeat**, or **for** loop, skipping to the next statement after the loop:

> *stat*   →   **break**

A **break** ends the innermost enclosing loop.

The **return** and **break** statements can only be written as the *last* statement of a block. If it is really necessary to **return** or **break** in the middle of a block, then an explicit inner block can be used, as in the idioms do return end and do break end, because now **return** and **break** are the last statements in their (inner) blocks.

2.4.5 For Statement

The **for** statement has two forms: one numeric and one generic.

The numeric **for** loop repeats a block of code while a control variable runs through an arithmetic progression. It has the following syntax:

> *stat*   →   **for** Name '=' *exp* ',' *exp* [',' *exp*] **do** *block* **end**

The *block* is repeated for *name* starting at the value of the first *exp*, until it passes the second *exp* by steps of the third *exp*. More precisely, a **for** statement like

```
for v = e1, e2, e3 do block end
```

is equivalent to the code:

```
do
   local var, limit, step = tonumber(e1), tonumber(e2), tonumber(e3)
   if not (var and limit and step) then error() end
   while (step > 0 and var <= limit) or (step <= 0 and var >= limit) do
     local v = var
     block
     var = var + step
   end
end
```

Note the following:

- All three control expressions are evaluated only once, before the loop starts. They must all result in numbers.

- *var*, *limit*, and *step* are invisible variables. The names are here for explanatory purposes only.

- If the third expression (the step) is absent, then a step of 1 is used.

- You can use **break** to exit a **for** loop.

- The loop variable v is local to the loop; you cannot use its value after the **for** ends or is broken. If you need this value, assign it to another variable before breaking or exiting the loop.

The generic **for** statement works over functions, called *iterators*. On each iteration, the iterator function is called to produce a new value, stopping when this new value is **nil**. The generic **for** loop has the following syntax:

$stat \quad \rightarrow \quad$ **for** *namelist* **in** *explist1* **do** *block* **end**
namelist $\quad \rightarrow \quad$ Name {',' Name}

A **for** statement like

```
for var_1, ···, var_n in explist do block end
```

is equivalent to the code:

```
do
   local f, s, var = explist
   while true do
     local var_1, ···, var_n = f(s, var)
     var = var_1
     if var == nil then break end
     block
   end
end
```

Note the following:

- *explist* is evaluated only once. Its results are an *iterator* function, a *state*, and an initial value for the first *iterator variable*.

- *f*, *s*, and *var* are invisible variables. The names are here for explanatory purposes only.

- You can use **break** to exit a **for** loop.

- The loop variables *var_i* are local to the loop; you cannot use their values after the **for** ends. If you need these values, then assign them to other variables before breaking or exiting the loop.

2.4.6 Function Calls as Statements

To allow possible side-effects, function calls can be executed as statements:

$stat \quad \rightarrow \quad functioncall$

In this case, all returned values are thrown away. Function calls are explained in §2.5.8.

2.4.7 Local Declarations

Local variables may be declared anywhere inside a block. The declaration may include an initial assignment:

$stat \quad \rightarrow \quad$ **local** *namelist* ['=' *explist1*]

If present, an initial assignment has the same semantics of a multiple assignment (see §2.4.3). Otherwise, all variables are initialized with **nil**.

A chunk is also a block (see §2.4.1), and so local variables can be declared in a chunk outside any explicit block. The scope of such local variables extends until the end of the chunk.

The visibility rules for local variables are explained in §2.6.

2.5 Expressions

The basic expressions in Lua are the following:

$$
\begin{array}{rcl}
\textit{exp} & \rightarrow & \textit{prefixexp} \\
\textit{exp} & \rightarrow & \textbf{nil} \mid \textbf{false} \mid \textbf{true} \\
\textit{exp} & \rightarrow & \text{Number} \\
\textit{exp} & \rightarrow & \text{String} \\
\textit{exp} & \rightarrow & \textit{function} \\
\textit{exp} & \rightarrow & \textit{tableconstructor} \\
\textit{exp} & \rightarrow & \text{`}\ldots\text{'} \\
\textit{exp} & \rightarrow & \textit{exp binop exp} \\
\textit{exp} & \rightarrow & \textit{unop exp} \\
\textit{prefixexp} & \rightarrow & \textit{var} \mid \textit{functioncall} \mid \text{`('} \textit{ exp } \text{')'}
\end{array}
$$

Numbers and literal strings are explained in §2.1; variables are explained in §2.3; function definitions are explained in §2.5.9; function calls are explained in §2.5.8; table constructors are explained in §2.5.7. Vararg expressions, denoted by three dots ('...'), can only be used inside vararg functions; they are explained in §2.5.9.

Binary operators comprise arithmetic operators (see §2.5.1), relational operators (see §2.5.2), logical operators (see §2.5.3), and the concatenation operator (see §2.5.4). Unary operators comprise the unary minus (see §2.5.1), the unary **not** (see §2.5.3), and the unary *length operator* (see §2.5.5).

Both function calls and vararg expressions may result in multiple values. If the expression is used as a statement (see §2.4.6) (only possible for function calls), then its return list is adjusted to zero elements, thus discarding all returned values. If the expression is used as the last (or the only) element of a list of expressions, then no adjustment is made (unless the call is enclosed in parentheses). In all other contexts, Lua adjusts the result list to one element, discarding all values except the first one.

Here are some examples:

```
f()                   -- adjusted to 0 results
g(f(), x)             -- f() is adjusted to 1 result
g(x, f())             -- g gets x plus all results from f()
a,b,c = f(), x        -- f() is adjusted to 1 result (c gets nil)
a,b = ...             -- a gets the first vararg parameter, b gets
                      -- the second (both a and b may get nil if there
                      -- is no corresponding vararg parameter)
```

```
a,b,c = x, f()      -- f() is adjusted to 2 results
a,b,c = f()         -- f() is adjusted to 3 results
return f()          -- returns all results from f()
return ...          -- returns all received vararg parameters
return x,y,f()      -- returns x, y, and all results from f()
{f()}               -- creates a list with all results from f()
{...}               -- creates a list with all vararg parameters
{f(), nil}          -- f() is adjusted to 1 result
```

An expression enclosed in parentheses always results in only one value. Thus, (f(x,y,z)) is always a single value, even if f returns several values. (The value of (f(x,y,z)) is the first value returned by f or **nil** if f does not return any values.)

2.5.1 Arithmetic Operators

Lua supports the usual arithmetic operators: the binary + (addition), - (subtraction), * (multiplication), / (division), % (modulo), and ^ (exponentiation); and unary - (negation). If the operands are numbers, or strings that can be converted to numbers (see §2.2.1), then all operations have the usual meaning. Exponentiation works for any exponent. For instance, x^(-0.5) computes the inverse of the square root of x. Modulo is defined as

```
a % b == a - math.floor(a/b)*b
```

That is, it is the remainder of a division that rounds the quotient towards minus infinity.

2.5.2 Relational Operators

The relational operators in Lua are

```
==    ~=    <    >    <=    >=
```

These operators always result in **false** or **true**.

Equality (==) first compares the type of its operands. If the types are different, then the result is **false**. Otherwise, the values of the operands are compared. Numbers and strings are compared in the usual way. Objects (tables, userdata, threads, and functions) are compared by *reference*: two objects are considered equal only if they are the *same* object. Every time you create a new object (a table, userdata, thread, or function), this new object is different from any previously existing object.

You can change the way that Lua compares tables and userdata by using the "eq" metamethod (see §2.8).

The conversion rules of §2.2.1 *do not* apply to equality comparisons. Thus, "0"==0 evaluates to **false**, and t[0] and t["0"] denote different entries in a table.

The operator ~= is exactly the negation of equality (==).

The order operators work as follows. If both arguments are numbers, then they are compared as such. Otherwise, if both arguments are strings, then their values are compared according to the current locale. Otherwise, Lua tries to call the "lt" or the "le" metamethod (see §2.8).

2.5.3   Logical Operators

The logical operators in Lua are **and**, **or**, and **not**. Like the control structures (see §2.4.4), all logical operators consider both **false** and **nil** as false and anything else as true.

The negation operator **not** always returns **false** or **true**. The conjunction operator **and** returns its first argument if this value is **false** or **nil**; otherwise, **and** returns its second argument. The disjunction operator **or** returns its first argument if this value is different from **nil** and **false**; otherwise, **or** returns its second argument. Both **and** and **or** use short-cut evaluation; that is, the second operand is evaluated only if necessary. Here are some examples:

```
10 or 20              → 10
10 or error()         → 10
nil or "a"            → "a"
nil and 10            → nil
false and error()     → false
false and nil         → false
false or nil          → nil
10 and 20             → 20
```

(In this manual, → indicates the result of the preceding expression.)

2.5.4   Concatenation

The string concatenation operator in Lua is denoted by two dots ('..'). If both operands are strings or numbers, then they are converted to strings according to the rules mentioned in §2.2.1. Otherwise, the "concat" metamethod is called (see §2.8).

2.5.5   The Length Operator

The length operator is denoted by the unary operator #. The length of a string is its number of bytes (that is, the usual meaning of string length when each character is one byte).

The length of a table t is defined to be any integer index n such that t[n] is not **nil** and t[n+1] is **nil**; moreover, if t[1] is **nil**, n may be zero. For a regular array, with non-nil values from 1 to a given n, its length is exactly that n, the index of its last value. If the array has "holes" (that is, **nil** values between other non-nil values), then #t may be any of the indices that directly precedes a **nil** value (that is, it may consider any such **nil** value as the end of the array).

2.5.6 Precedence

Operator precedence in Lua follows the table below, from lower to higher priority:

```
or
and
<      >      <=     >=     ~=     ==
..
+      -
*      /      %
not    #      -  (unary)
^
```

As usual, you can use parentheses to change the precedences of an expression. The concatenation ('..') and exponentiation ('^') operators are right associative. All other binary operators are left associative.

2.5.7 Table Constructors

Table constructors are expressions that create tables. Every time a constructor is evaluated, a new table is created. Constructors can be used to create empty tables, or to create a table and initialize some of its fields. The general syntax for constructors is

$$
\begin{aligned}
\textit{tableconstructor} \quad &\rightarrow \quad \text{'\{' } [\textit{fieldlist}] \text{ '\}'} \\
\textit{fieldlist} \quad &\rightarrow \quad \textit{field } \{\textit{fieldsep field}\} \, [\textit{fieldsep}] \\
\textit{field} \quad &\rightarrow \quad \text{'['} \textit{exp} \text{']' '='} \textit{exp} \mid \text{Name '='} \textit{exp} \mid \textit{exp} \\
\textit{fieldsep} \quad &\rightarrow \quad \text{',' } \mid \text{ ';'}
\end{aligned}
$$

Each field of the form [exp1] = exp2 adds to the new table an entry with key exp1 and value exp2. A field of the form name = exp is equivalent to ["name"] = exp. Finally, fields of the form exp are equivalent to [i] = exp, where i are consecutive numerical integers, starting with 1. Fields in the other formats do not affect this counting. For example,

```
a = { [f(1)] = g; "x", "y"; x = 1, f(x), [30] = 23; 45 }
```

is equivalent to

```
do
  local t = {}
  t[f(1)] = g
  t[1] = "x"          -- 1st exp
  t[2] = "y"          -- 2nd exp
  t.x = 1             -- t["x"] = 1
  t[3] = f(x)         -- 3rd exp
  t[30] = 23
  t[4] = 45           -- 4th exp
  a = t
end
```

If the last field in the list has the form exp and the expression is a function call or a vararg expression, then all values returned by this expression enter the list consecutively (see §2.5.8). To avoid this, enclose the function call (or the vararg expression) in parentheses (see §2.5).

The field list may have an optional trailing separator, as a convenience for machine-generated code.

2.5.8   Function Calls

A function call in Lua has the following syntax:

functioncall   →   *prefixexp args*

In a function call, first *prefixexp* and *args* are evaluated. If the value of *prefixexp* has type *function*, then this function is called with the given arguments. Otherwise, the *prefixexp* "call" metamethod is called, having as first parameter the value of *prefixexp*, followed by the original call arguments (see §2.8).

The form

functioncall   →   *prefixexp* ':' Name *args*

can be used to call "methods". A call v:name(*args*) is syntactic sugar for v.name(v,*args*), except that v is evaluated only once.

Arguments have the following syntax:

args   →   '(' [*explist1*] ')'
args   →   *tableconstructor*
args   →   String

All argument expressions are evaluated before the call. A call of the form f{*fields*} is syntactic sugar for f({*fields*}); that is, the argument list is a single new table. A call of the form f'*string*' (or f"*string*" or f[[*string*]]) is syntactic sugar for f('*string*'); that is, the argument list is a single literal string.

As an exception to the free-format syntax of Lua, you cannot put a line break before the '(' in a function call. This restriction avoids some ambiguities in the language. If you write

```
a = f
(g).x(a)
```

Lua would see that as a single statement, a=f(g).x(a). So, if you want two statements, you must add a semi-colon between them. If you actually want to call f, you must remove the line break before (g).

A call of the form return *functioncall* is called a *tail call*. Lua implements *proper tail calls* (or *proper tail recursion*): in a tail call, the called function reuses the stack entry of the calling function. Therefore, there is no limit on the number of nested tail calls that a program can execute. However, a tail call erases any debug information about the calling function. Note that a tail call only happens with a particular syntax, where the **return** has one single function call as argument; this syntax makes the calling function return exactly the returns of the called function. So, none of the following examples are tail calls:

```
return (f(x))       -- results adjusted to 1
return 2 * f(x)
return x, f(x)      -- additional results
f(x); return        -- results discarded
return x or f(x)    -- results adjusted to 1
```

2.5.9 Function Definitions

The syntax for function definition is

$function \quad \rightarrow \quad$ **function** $funcbody$
$funcbody \quad \rightarrow \quad$ '(' [$parlist1$] ')' $block$ **end**

The following syntactic sugar simplifies function definitions:

$stat \quad \rightarrow \quad$ **function** $funcname\ funcbody$
$stat \quad \rightarrow \quad$ **local function** Name $funcbody$
$funcname \quad \rightarrow \quad$ Name {'.' Name} [':' Name]

The statement

```
function f () body end
```

translates to

```
f = function () body end
```

The statement

```
function t.a.b.c.f () body end
```

translates to

```
t.a.b.c.f = function () body end
```

The statement

```
local function f () body end
```

translates to

```
local f; f = function () body end
```

not to

```
local f = function () body end
```

(This only makes a difference when the body of the function contains references to f.)

A function definition is an executable expression, whose value has type *function*. When Lua pre-compiles a chunk, all its function bodies are pre-compiled too. Then, whenever Lua executes the function definition, the function

is *instantiated* (or *closed*). This function instance (or *closure*) is the final value of
the expression. Different instances of the same function may refer to different
external local variables and may have different environment tables.

Parameters act as local variables that are initialized with the argument
values:

    parlist1   →   *namelist* [',' '...'] | '...'

When a function is called, the list of arguments is adjusted to the length of the
list of parameters, unless the function is a variadic or *vararg function*, which is
indicated by three dots ('...') at the end of its parameter list. A vararg function
does not adjust its argument list; instead, it collects all extra arguments and
supplies them to the function through a *vararg expression*, which is also written
as three dots. The value of this expression is a list of all actual extra arguments,
similar to a function with multiple results. If a vararg expression is used inside
another expression or in the middle of a list of expressions, then its return list
is adjusted to one element. If the expression is used as the last element of a
list of expressions, then no adjustment is made (unless the call is enclosed in
parentheses).

As an example, consider the following definitions:

```
function f(a, b) end
function g(a, b, ...) end
function r() return 1,2,3 end
```

Then, we have the following mapping from arguments to parameters and to the
vararg expression:

```
CALL                PARAMETERS

f(3)                a=3, b=nil
f(3, 4)             a=3, b=4
f(3, 4, 5)          a=3, b=4
f(r(), 10)          a=1, b=10
f(r())              a=1, b=2

g(3)                a=3, b=nil, ...  →   (nothing)
g(3, 4)             a=3, b=4,   ...  →   (nothing)
g(3, 4, 5, 8)       a=3, b=4,   ...  →   5  8
g(5, r())           a=5, b=1,   ...  →   2  3
```

Results are returned using the **return** statement (see §2.4.4). If control
reaches the end of a function without encountering a **return** statement, then
the function returns with no results.

The *colon* syntax is used for defining *methods*, that is, functions that have an
implicit extra parameter self. Thus, the statement

```
function t.a.b.c:f (params) body end
```

is syntactic sugar for

```
t.a.b.c.f = function (self, params) body end
```

2.6 Visibility Rules

Lua is a lexically scoped language. The scope of variables begins at the first statement *after* their declaration and lasts until the end of the innermost block that includes the declaration. Consider the following example:

```
x = 10                  -- global variable
do                      -- new block
  local x = x           -- new 'x', with value 10
  print(x)              → 10
  x = x+1
  do                    -- another block
    local x = x+1       -- another 'x'
    print(x)            → 12
  end
  print(x)              → 11
end
print(x)                → 10   (the global one)
```

Notice that, in a declaration like local x=x, the new x being declared is not in scope yet, and so the second x refers to the outside variable.

Because of the lexical scoping rules, local variables can be freely accessed by functions defined inside their scope. A local variable used by an inner function is called an *upvalue*, or *external local variable*, inside the inner function.

Notice that each execution of a **local** statement defines new local variables. Consider the following example:

```
a = {}
local x = 20
for i=1,10 do
  local y = 0
  a[i] = function () y=y+1; return x+y end
end
```

The loop creates ten closures (that is, ten instances of the anonymous function). Each of these closures uses a different y variable, while all of them share the same x.

2.7 Error Handling

Because Lua is an embedded extension language, all Lua actions start from C code in the host program calling a function from the Lua library (see lua_pcall on page 40). Whenever an error occurs during Lua compilation or execution, control returns to C, which can take appropriate measures (such as printing an error message).

Lua code can explicitly generate an error by calling the error function. If you need to catch errors in Lua, you can use the pcall function.

2.8   Metatables

Every value in Lua may have a *metatable*. This *metatable* is an ordinary
Lua table that defines the behavior of the original value under certain special
operations. You can change several aspects of the behavior of operations over
a value by setting specific fields in its metatable. For instance, when a non-
numeric value is the operand of an addition, Lua checks for a function in the
field "__add" in its metatable. If it finds one, Lua calls this function to perform
the addition.

We call the keys in a metatable *events* and the values *metamethods*. In the
previous example, the event is "add" and the metamethod is the function that
performs the addition.

You can query the metatable of any value through the getmetatable function.

You can replace the metatable of tables through the setmetatable function.
You cannot change the metatable of other types from Lua (except using the
debug library); you must use the C API for that.

Tables and userdata have individual metatables (although multiple tables
and userdata can share a same table as their metatable); values of all other
types share one single metatable per type. So, there is one single metatable for
all numbers, and for all strings, etc.

A metatable may control how an object behaves in arithmetic operations,
order comparisons, concatenation, length operation, and indexing. A metatable
can also define a function to be called when a userdata is garbage collected. For
each of these operations Lua associates a specific key called an *event*. When Lua
performs one of these operations over a value, it checks whether this value has
a metatable with the corresponding event. If so, the value associated with that
key (the metamethod) controls how Lua will perform the operation.

Metatables control the operations listed next. Each operation is identified by
its corresponding name. The key for each operation is a string with its name
prefixed by two underscores, '__'; for instance, the key for operation "add" is the
string "__add". The semantics of these operations is better explained by a Lua
function describing how the interpreter executes the operation.

The code shown here in Lua is only illustrative; the real behavior is hard
coded in the interpreter and it is much more efficient than this simulation.
All functions used in these descriptions (rawget, tonumber, etc.) are described
in §5.1. In particular, to retrieve the metamethod of a given object, we use the
expression

```
metatable(obj)[event]
```

This should be read as

```
rawget(getmetatable(obj) or {}, event)
```

That is, the access to a metamethod does not invoke other metamethods, and the access to objects with no metatables does not fail (it simply results in **nil**).

"add": the + operation.

The function getbinhandler below defines how Lua chooses a handler for a binary operation. First, Lua tries the first operand. If its type does not define a handler for the operation, then Lua tries the second operand.

```
function getbinhandler (op1, op2, event)
  return metatable(op1)[event] or metatable(op2)[event]
end
```

By using this function, the behavior of the op1+op2 is

```
function add_event (op1, op2)
  local o1, o2 = tonumber(op1), tonumber(op2)
  if o1 and o2 then   -- both operands are numeric?
    return o1 + o2    -- '+' here is the primitive 'add'
  else -- at least one of the operands is not numeric
    local h = getbinhandler(op1, op2, "__add")
    if h then
      -- call the handler with both operands
      return h(op1, op2)
    else  -- no handler available: default behavior
      error(···)
    end
  end
end
```

"sub": the - operation. Behavior similar to the "add" operation.

"mul": the * operation. Behavior similar to the "add" operation.

"div": the / operation. Behavior similar to the "add" operation.

"mod": the % operation. Behavior similar to the "add" operation, with the operation o1-floor(o1/o2)*o2 as the primitive operation.

"pow": the ˆ (exponentiation) operation. Behavior similar to the "add" operation, with the function pow (from the C math library) as the primitive operation.

"unm": the unary - operation.

```
function unm_event (op)
  local o = tonumber(op)
  if o then  -- operand is numeric?
    return -o  -- '-' here is the primitive 'unm'
  else  -- the operand is not numeric.
    -- Try to get a handler from the operand
    local h = metatable(op).__unm
    if h then
      -- call the handler with the operand
      return h(op)
    else  -- no handler available: default behavior
      error(···)
    end
  end
end
```

"concat": the .. (concatenation) operation.

```
function concat_event (op1, op2)
  if (type(op1) == "string" or type(op1) == "number") and
     (type(op2) == "string" or type(op2) == "number") then
    return op1 .. op2  -- primitive string concatenation
  else
    local h = getbinhandler(op1, op2, "__concat")
    if h then
      return h(op1, op2)
    else
      error(···)
    end
  end
end
```

"len": the # operation.

```
function len_event (op)
  if type(op) == "string" then
    return strlen(op)          -- primitive string length
  elseif type(op) == "table" then
    return #op                 -- primitive table length
  else
    local h = metatable(op).__len
    if h then
      -- call the handler with the operand
      return h(op)
    else  -- no handler available: default behavior
      error(···)
    end
  end
end
```

See §2.5.5 for a description of the length of a table.

"eq": the == operation. The function getcomphandler defines how Lua chooses a metamethod for comparison operators. A metamethod only is selected when both objects being compared have the same type and the same meta-method for the selected operation.

```
function getcomphandler (op1, op2, event)
  if type(op1) ~= type(op2) then return nil end
  local mm1 = metatable(op1)[event]
  local mm2 = metatable(op2)[event]
  if mm1 == mm2 then return mm1 else return nil end
end
```

The "eq" event is defined as follows:

```
function eq_event (op1, op2)
  if type(op1) ~= type(op2) then   -- different types?
    return false    -- different objects
  end
  if op1 == op2 then    -- primitive equal?
    return true    -- objects are equal
  end
  -- try metamethod
  local h = getcomphandler(op1, op2, "__eq")
  if h then
    return h(op1, op2)
  else
    return false
  end
end
```

a~=b is equivalent to not (a==b).

"lt": the < operation.

```
function lt_event (op1, op2)
  if type(op1) == "number" and type(op2) == "number" then
    return op1 < op2    -- numeric comparison
  elseif type(op1) == "string" and type(op2) == "string" then
    return op1 < op2    -- lexicographic comparison
  else
    local h = getcomphandler(op1, op2, "__lt")
    if h then
      return h(op1, op2)
    else
      error(···);
    end
  end
end
```

a > b is equivalent to b < a.

"le": the <= operation.

```
function le_event (op1, op2)
  if type(op1) == "number" and type(op2) == "number" then
    return op1 <= op2    -- numeric comparison
  elseif type(op1) == "string" and type(op2) == "string" then
    return op1 <= op2    -- lexicographic comparison
  else
    local h = getcomphandler(op1, op2, "__le")
    if h then
      return h(op1, op2)
    else
      h = getcomphandler(op1, op2, "__lt")
      if h then
        return not h(op2, op1)
      else
        error(···);
      end
    end
  end
end
```

a >= b is equivalent to b <= a. Note that, in the absence of a "le" metamethod, Lua tries the "lt", assuming that a <= b is equivalent to not (b < a).

"index": The indexing access table[key].

```
function gettable_event (table, key)
  local h
  if type(table) == "table" then
    local v = rawget(table, key)
    if v ~= nil then return v end
    h = metatable(table).__index
    if h == nil then return nil end
  else
    h = metatable(table).__index
    if h == nil then
      error(···);
    end
  end
  if type(h) == "function" then
    return h(table, key)      -- call the handler
  else return h[key]          -- or repeat operation on it
  end
end
```

"newindex": The indexing assignment table[key] = value.

```
function settable_event (table, key, value)
  local h
  if type(table) == "table" then
    local v = rawget(table, key)
    if v ~= nil then rawset(table, key, value); return end
    h = metatable(table).__newindex
    if h == nil then rawset(table, key, value); return end
  else
    h = metatable(table).__newindex
    if h == nil then
      error(···);
    end
  end
  if type(h) == "function" then
    return h(table, key,value)    -- call the handler
  else h[key] = value             -- or repeat operation on it
  end
end
```

"call": called when Lua calls a value.

```
function function_event (func, ...)
  if type(func) == "function" then
    return func(...)   -- primitive call
  else
    local h = metatable(func).__call
    if h then
      return h(func, ...)
    else
      error(···)
    end
  end
end
```

2.9 Environments

Besides metatables, objects of types thread, function, and userdata have another table associated with them, called their *environment*. Like metatables, environments are regular tables and multiple objects can share the same environment.

Environments associated with userdata have no meaning for Lua. It is only a convenience feature for programmers to associate a table to a userdata.

Environments associated with threads are called *global environments*. They are used as the default environment for their threads and non-nested functions created by the thread (through loadfile, loadstring or load) and can be directly accessed by C code (see §3.3).

Environments associated with C functions can be directly accessed by C code (see §3.3). They are used as the default environment for other C functions created by the function.

Environments associated with Lua functions are used to resolve all accesses to global variables within the function (see §2.3). They are used as the default environment for other Lua functions created by the function.

You can change the environment of a Lua function or the running thread by calling setfenv. You can get the environment of a Lua function or the running thread by calling getfenv. To manipulate the environment of other objects (userdata, C functions, other threads) you must use the C API.

2.10   Garbage Collection

Lua performs automatic memory management. This means that you have to worry neither about allocating memory for new objects nor about freeing it when the objects are no longer needed. Lua manages memory automatically by running a *garbage collector* from time to time to collect all *dead objects* (that is, these objects that are no longer accessible from Lua). All objects in Lua are subject to automatic management: tables, userdata, functions, threads, and strings.

Lua implements an incremental mark-and-sweep collector. It uses two numbers to control its garbage-collection cycles: the *garbage-collector pause* and the *garbage-collector step multiplier*.

The garbage-collector pause controls how long the collector waits before starting a new cycle. Larger values make the collector less aggressive. Values smaller than 1 mean the collector will not wait to start a new cycle. A value of 2 means that the collector waits for the total memory in use to double before starting a new cycle.

The step multiplier controls the relative speed of the collector relative to memory allocation. Larger values make the collector more aggressive but also increase the size of each incremental step. Values smaller than 1 make the collector too slow and may result in the collector never finishing a cycle. The default, 2, means that the collector runs at "twice" the speed of memory allocation.

You can change these numbers by calling lua_gc in C or collectgarbage in Lua. Both get percentage points as arguments (so an argument of 100 means a real value of 1). With these functions you can also control the collector directly (e.g., stop and restart it).

2.10.1   Garbage-Collection Metamethods

Using the C API, you can set garbage-collector metamethods for userdata (see §2.8). These metamethods are also called *finalizers*. Finalizers allow you to coordinate Lua's garbage collection with external resource management (such as closing files, network or database connections, or freeing your own memory).

Garbage userdata with a field __gc in their metatables are not collected immediately by the garbage collector. Instead, Lua puts them in a list. After the collection, Lua does the equivalent of the following function for each userdata in that list:

```
function gc_event (udata)
  local h = metatable(udata).__gc
  if h then
    h(udata)
  end
end
```

At the end of each garbage-collection cycle, the finalizers for userdata are called in *reverse* order of their creation, among those collected in that cycle. That is, the first finalizer to be called is the one associated with the userdata created last in the program.

2.10.2 Weak Tables

A *weak table* is a table whose elements are *weak references*. A weak reference is ignored by the garbage collector. In other words, if the only references to an object are weak references, then the garbage collector will collect this object.

A weak table can have weak keys, weak values, or both. A table with weak keys allows the collection of its keys, but prevents the collection of its values. A table with both weak keys and weak values allows the collection of both keys and values. In any case, if either the key or the value is collected, the whole pair is removed from the table. The weakness of a table is controlled by the value of the __mode field of its metatable. If the __mode field is a string containing the character 'k', the keys in the table are weak. If __mode contains 'v', the values in the table are weak.

After you use a table as a metatable, you should not change the value of its field __mode. Otherwise, the weak behavior of the tables controlled by this metatable is undefined.

2.11 Coroutines

Lua supports coroutines, also called *collaborative multithreading*. A coroutine in Lua represents an independent thread of execution. Unlike threads in multithread systems, however, a coroutine only suspends its execution by explicitly calling a yield function.

You create a coroutine with a call to coroutine.create. Its sole argument is a function that is the main function of the coroutine. The create function only creates a new coroutine and returns a handle to it (an object of type *thread*); it does not start the coroutine execution.

When you first call coroutine.resume, passing as its first argument the thread returned by coroutine.create, the coroutine starts its execution, at the first line of its main function. Extra arguments passed to coroutine.resume are passed on to the coroutine main function. After the coroutine starts running, it runs until it terminates or *yields*.

A coroutine can terminate its execution in two ways: normally, when its main function returns (explicitly or implicitly, after the last instruction); and abnormally, if there is an unprotected error. In the first case, `coroutine.resume` returns **true**, plus any values returned by the coroutine main function. In case of errors, `coroutine.resume` returns **false** plus an error message.

A coroutine yields by calling `coroutine.yield`. When a coroutine yields, the corresponding `coroutine.resume` returns immediately, even if the yield happens inside nested function calls (that is, not in the main function, but in a function directly or indirectly called by the main function). In the case of a yield, `coroutine.resume` also returns **true**, plus any values passed to `coroutine.yield`. The next time you resume the same coroutine, it continues its execution from the point where it yielded, with the call to `coroutine.yield` returning any extra arguments passed to `coroutine.resume`.

Like `coroutine.create`, the `coroutine.wrap` function also creates a coroutine, but instead of returning the coroutine itself, it returns a function that, when called, resumes the coroutine. Any arguments passed to this function go as extra arguments to `coroutine.resume`. `coroutine.wrap` returns all the values returned by `coroutine.resume`, except the first one (the boolean error code). Unlike `coroutine.resume`, `coroutine.wrap` does not catch errors; any error is propagated to the caller.

As an example, consider the following code:

```
function foo (a)
  print("foo", a)
  return coroutine.yield(2*a)
end

co = coroutine.create(function (a,b)
      print("co-body", a, b)
      local r = foo(a+1)
      print("co-body", r)
      local r, s = coroutine.yield(a+b, a-b)
      print("co-body", r, s)
      return b, "end"
end)

print("main", coroutine.resume(co, 1, 10))
print("main", coroutine.resume(co, "r"))
print("main", coroutine.resume(co, "x", "y"))
print("main", coroutine.resume(co, "x", "y"))
```

When you run it, it produces the following output:

```
co-body 1        10
foo     2
```

```
main     true    4
co-body  r
main     true    11      -9
co-body  x       y
main     true    10      end
main     false   cannot resume dead coroutine
```

3   The Application Program Interface

This section describes the C API for Lua, that is, the set of C functions available to the host program to communicate with Lua. All API functions and related types and constants are declared in the header file `lua.h`.

Even when we use the term "function", any facility in the API may be provided as a macro instead. All such macros use each of their arguments exactly once (except for the first argument, which is always a Lua state), and so do not generate any hidden side-effects.

As in most C libraries, the Lua API functions do not check their arguments for validity or consistency. However, you can change this behavior by compiling Lua with a proper definition for the macro `luai_apicheck`, in file `luaconf.h`.

3.1   The Stack

Lua uses a *virtual stack* to pass values to and from C. Each element in this stack represents a Lua value (**nil**, number, string, etc.).

Whenever Lua calls C, the called function gets a new stack, which is independent of previous stacks and of stacks of C functions that are still active. This stack initially contains any arguments to the C function and it is where the C function pushes its results to be returned to the caller (see `lua_CFunction` on page 32).

For convenience, most query operations in the API do not follow a strict stack discipline. Instead, they can refer to any element in the stack by using an *index*: A positive index represents an *absolute* stack position (starting at 1); a negative index represents an *offset* relative to the top of the stack. More specifically, if the stack has n elements, then index 1 represents the first element (that is, the element that was pushed onto the stack first) and index n represents the last element; index –1 also represents the last element (that is, the element at the top) and index $-n$ represents the first element. We say that an index is *valid* if it lies between 1 and the stack top (that is, if $1 \leq \text{abs(index)} \leq \text{top}$).

3.2   Stack Size

When you interact with Lua API, you are responsible for ensuring consistency. In particular, *you are responsible for controlling stack overflow*. You can use the function `lua_checkstack` to grow the stack size.

Whenever Lua calls C, it ensures that at least `LUA_MINSTACK` stack positions are available. `LUA_MINSTACK` is defined as 20, so that usually you do not have to worry about stack space unless your code has loops pushing elements onto the stack.

Most query functions accept as indices any value inside the available stack space, that is, indices up to the maximum stack size you have set through `lua_checkstack`. Such indices are called *acceptable indices*. More formally, we define an *acceptable index* as follows:

```
(index < 0 && abs(index) <= top) ||
(index > 0 && index <= stackspace)
```

Note that 0 is never an acceptable index.

3.3 Pseudo-Indices

Unless otherwise noted, any function that accepts valid indices can also be called with *pseudo-indices*, which represent some Lua values that are accessible to C code but which are not in the stack. Pseudo-indices are used to access the thread environment, the function environment, the registry, and the upvalues of a C function (see §3.4).

The thread environment (where global variables live) is always at pseudo-index LUA_GLOBALSINDEX. The environment of the running C function is always at pseudo-index LUA_ENVIRONINDEX.

To access and change the value of global variables, you can use regular table operations over an environment table. For instance, to access the value of a global variable, do

```
lua_getfield(L, LUA_GLOBALSINDEX, varname);
```

3.4 C Closures

When a C function is created, it is possible to associate some values with it, thus creating a *C closure*; these values are called *upvalues* and are accessible to the function whenever it is called (see lua_pushcclosure on page 41).

Whenever a C function is called, its upvalues are located at specific pseudo-indices. These pseudo-indices are produced by the macro lua_upvalueindex. The first value associated with a function is at position lua_upvalueindex(1), and so on. Any access to lua_upvalueindex(n), where n is greater than the number of upvalues of the current function, produces an acceptable (but invalid) index.

3.5 Registry

Lua provides a *registry*, a pre-defined table that can be used by any C code to store whatever Lua value it needs to store. This table is always located at pseudo-index LUA_REGISTRYINDEX. Any C library can store data into this table, but it should take care to choose keys different from those used by other libraries, to avoid collisions. Typically, you should use as key a string containing your library name or a light userdata with the address of a C object in your code.

The integer keys in the registry are used by the reference mechanism, implemented by the auxiliary library, and therefore should not be used for other purposes.

3.6 Error Handling in C

Internally, Lua uses the C `longjmp` facility to handle errors. (You can also choose to use exceptions if you use C++; see file `luaconf.h`.) When Lua faces any error (such as memory allocation errors, type errors, syntax errors, and runtime errors) it *raises* an error; that is, it does a long jump. A *protected environment* uses `setjmp` to set a recover point; any error jumps to the most recent active recover point.

Almost any function in the API may raise an error, for instance due to a memory allocation error. The following functions run in protected mode (that is, they create a protected environment to run), so they never raise an error: `lua_newstate`, `lua_close`, `lua_load`, `lua_pcall`, and `lua_cpcall`.

Inside a C function you can raise an error by calling `lua_error`.

3.7 Functions and Types

Here we list all functions and types from the C API in alphabetical order.

lua_Alloc

```
typedef void * (*lua_Alloc) (void *ud,
                             void *ptr,
                             size_t osize,
                             size_t nsize);
```

The type of the memory-allocation function used by Lua states. The allocator function must provide a functionality similar to `realloc`, but not exactly the same. Its arguments are ud, an opaque pointer passed to `lua_newstate`; ptr, a pointer to the block being allocated/reallocated/freed; osize, the original size of the block; nsize, the new size of the block. ptr is NULL if and only if osize is zero. When nsize is zero, the allocator must return NULL; if osize is not zero, it should free the block pointed to by ptr. When nsize is not zero, the allocator returns NULL if and only if it cannot fill the request. When nsize is not zero and osize is zero, the allocator should behave like `malloc`. When nsize and osize are not zero, the allocator behaves like `realloc`. Lua assumes that the allocator never fails when osize>=nsize.

Here is a simple implementation for the allocator function. It is used in the auxiliary library by `luaL_newstate`.

```
static void *l_alloc (void *ud, void *ptr, size_t osize,
                                            size_t nsize) {
  (void)ud;  (void)osize;  /* not used */
  if (nsize == 0) {
    free(ptr);
    return NULL;
  }
  else
    return realloc(ptr, nsize);
}
```

This code assumes that free(NULL) has no effect and that realloc(NULL, size) is equivalent to malloc(size). ANSI C ensures both behaviors.

lua_atpanic

```
lua_CFunction lua_atpanic (lua_State *L, lua_CFunction panicf);
```

Sets a new panic function and returns the old one.

If an error happens outside any protected environment, Lua calls a *panic function* and then calls exit(EXIT_FAILURE), thus exiting the host application. Your panic function may avoid this exit by never returning (e.g., doing a long jump).

The panic function can access the error message at the top of the stack.

lua_call

```
void lua_call (lua_State *L, int nargs, int nresults);
```

Calls a function.

To call a function you must use the following protocol: first, the function to be called is pushed onto the stack; then, the arguments to the function are pushed in direct order; that is, the first argument is pushed first. Finally you call lua_call; nargs is the number of arguments that you pushed onto the stack. All arguments and the function value are popped from the stack when the function is called. The function results are pushed onto the stack when the function returns. The number of results is adjusted to nresults, unless nresults is LUA_MULTRET. In this case, *all* results from the function are pushed. Lua takes care that the returned values fit into the stack space. The function results are pushed onto the stack in direct order (the first result is pushed first), so that after the call the last result is on the top of the stack.

Any error inside the called function is propagated upwards (with a longjmp).

The following example shows how the host program may do the equivalent to this Lua code:

```
a = f("how", t.x, 14)
```

Here it is in C:

```
lua_getfield(L, LUA_GLOBALSINDEX, "f"); /* function to be called */
lua_pushstring(L, "how");                       /* 1st argument */
lua_getfield(L, LUA_GLOBALSINDEX, "t");   /* table to be indexed */
lua_getfield(L, -1, "x");         /* push result of t.x (2nd arg) */
lua_remove(L, -2);                     /* remove 't' from the stack */
lua_pushinteger(L, 14);                         /* 3rd argument */
lua_call(L, 3, 1);     /* call 'f' with 3 arguments and 1 result */
lua_setfield(L, LUA_GLOBALSINDEX, "a");         /* set global 'a' */
```

Note that the code above is "balanced": at its end, the stack is back to its original configuration. This is considered good programming practice.

lua_CFunction

```
typedef int (*lua_CFunction) (lua_State *L);
```

Type for C functions.

In order to communicate properly with Lua, a C function must use the following protocol, which defines the way parameters and results are passed: a C function receives its arguments from Lua in its stack in direct order (the first argument is pushed first). So, when the function starts, lua_gettop(L) returns the number of arguments received by the function. The first argument (if any) is at index 1 and its last argument is at index lua_gettop(L). To return values to Lua, a C function just pushes them onto the stack, in direct order (the first result is pushed first), and returns the number of results. Any other value in the stack below the results will be properly discarded by Lua. Like a Lua function, a C function called by Lua can also return many results.

As an example, the following function receives a variable number of numerical arguments and returns their average and sum:

```c
static int foo (lua_State *L) {
  int n = lua_gettop(L);      /* number of arguments */
  lua_Number sum = 0;
  int i;
  for (i = 1; i <= n; i++) {
    if (!lua_isnumber(L, i)) {
      lua_pushstring(L, "incorrect argument");
      lua_error(L);
    }
    sum += lua_tonumber(L, i);
  }
  lua_pushnumber(L, sum/n);        /* first result */
  lua_pushnumber(L, sum);          /* second result */
  return 2;                    /* number of results */
}
```

lua_checkstack

```
int lua_checkstack (lua_State *L, int extra);
```

Ensures that there are at least extra free stack slots in the stack. It returns false if it cannot grow the stack to that size. This function never shrinks the stack; if the stack is already larger than the new size, it is left unchanged.

lua_close

```
void lua_close (lua_State *L);
```

Destroys all objects in the given Lua state (calling the corresponding garbage-collection metamethods, if any) and frees all dynamic memory used by this state. On several platforms, you may not need to call this function, because all resources are naturally released when the host program ends. On the other hand, long-running programs, such as a daemon or a web server, might need to release states as soon as they are not needed, to avoid growing too large.

lua_concat

```
void lua_concat (lua_State *L, int n);
```

Concatenates the n values at the top of the stack, pops them, and leaves the result at the top. If n is 1, the result is the single string on the stack (that is, the function does nothing); if n is 0, the result is the empty string. Concatenation is done following the usual semantics of Lua (see §2.5.4).

lua_cpcall

```
int lua_cpcall (lua_State *L, lua_CFunction func, void *ud);
```

Calls the C function func in protected mode. func starts with only one element in its stack, a light userdata containing ud. In case of errors, lua_cpcall returns the same error codes as lua_pcall, plus the error object on the top of the stack; otherwise, it returns zero, and does not change the stack. All values returned by func are discarded.

lua_createtable

```
void lua_createtable (lua_State *L, int narr, int nrec);
```

Creates a new empty table and pushes it onto the stack. The new table has space pre-allocated for narr array elements and nrec non-array elements. This pre-allocation is useful when you know exactly how many elements the table will have. Otherwise you can use the function lua_newtable.

lua_dump

```
int lua_dump (lua_State *L, lua_Writer writer, void *data);
```

Dumps a function as a binary chunk. Receives a Lua function on the top of the stack and produces a binary chunk that, if loaded again, results in a function equivalent to the one dumped. As it produces parts of the chunk, lua_dump calls function writer (see lua_Writer on page 48) with the given data to write them.

The value returned is the error code returned by the last call to the writer; 0 means no errors.

This function does not pop the Lua function from the stack.

lua_equal

```
int lua_equal (lua_State *L, int index1, int index2);
```

Returns 1 if the two values in acceptable indices `index1` and `index2` are equal, following the semantics of the Lua == operator (that is, may call metamethods). Otherwise returns 0. Also returns 0 if any of the indices is non valid.

lua_error

```
int lua_error (lua_State *L);
```

Generates a Lua error. The error message (which can actually be a Lua value of any type) must be on the stack top. This function does a long jump, and therefore never returns. (see `luaL_error` on page 59).

lua_gc

```
int lua_gc (lua_State *L, int what, int data);
```

Controls the garbage collector.

This function performs several tasks, according to the value of the parameter `what`:

`LUA_GCSTOP`: stops the garbage collector.

`LUA_GCRESTART`: restarts the garbage collector.

`LUA_GCCOLLECT`: performs a full garbage-collection cycle.

`LUA_GCCOUNT`: returns the current amount of memory (in Kbytes) in use by Lua.

`LUA_GCCOUNTB`: returns the remainder of dividing the current amount of bytes of memory in use by Lua by 1024.

`LUA_GCSTEP`: performs an incremental step of garbage collection. The step "size" is controlled by `data` (larger values mean more steps) in a non-specified way. If you want to control the step size you must experimentally tune the value of `data`. The function returns 1 if the step finished a garbage-collection cycle.

`LUA_GCSETPAUSE`: sets `data`/100 as the new value for the *pause* of the collector (see §2.10). The function returns the previous value of the pause.

`LUA_GCSETSTEPMUL`: sets `arg`/100 as the new value for the *step multiplier* of the collector (see §2.10). The function returns the previous value of the step multiplier.

lua_getallocf

```
lua_Alloc lua_getallocf (lua_State *L, void **ud);
```

Returns the memory-allocation function of a given state. If ud is not NULL, Lua stores in *ud the opaque pointer passed to lua_newstate.

lua_getfenv

```
void lua_getfenv (lua_State *L, int index);
```

Pushes onto the stack the environment table of the value at the given index.

lua_getfield

```
void lua_getfield (lua_State *L, int index, const char *k);
```

Pushes onto the stack the value t[k], where t is the value at the given valid index index. As in Lua, this function may trigger a metamethod for the "index" event (see §2.8).

lua_getglobal

```
void lua_getglobal (lua_State *L, const char *name);
```

Pushes onto the stack the value of the global name. It is defined as a macro:

```
#define lua_getglobal(L,s)  lua_getfield(L, LUA_GLOBALSINDEX, s)
```

lua_getmetatable

```
int lua_getmetatable (lua_State *L, int index);
```

Pushes onto the stack the metatable of the value at the given acceptable index. If the index is not valid, or if the value does not have a metatable, the function returns 0 and pushes nothing on the stack.

lua_gettable

```
void lua_gettable (lua_State *L, int index);
```

Pushes onto the stack the value t[k], where t is the value at the given valid index index and k is the value at the top of the stack.

This function pops the key from the stack (putting the resulting value in its place). As in Lua, this function may trigger a metamethod for the "index" event (see §2.8).

lua_gettop

```
int lua_gettop (lua_State *L);
```

Returns the index of the top element in the stack. Because indices start at 1, this result is equal to the number of elements in the stack (and so 0 means an empty stack).

lua_insert

```
void lua_insert (lua_State *L, int index);
```

Moves the top element into the given valid index, shifting up the elements above this index to open space. Cannot be called with a pseudo-index, because a pseudo-index is not an actual stack position.

lua_Integer

```
typedef ptrdiff_t lua_Integer;
```

The type used by the Lua API to represent integral values.

By default it is a `ptrdiff_t`, which is usually the largest integral type the machine handles "comfortably".

lua_isboolean

```
int lua_isboolean (lua_State *L, int index);
```

Returns 1 if the value at the given acceptable index has type boolean, and 0 otherwise.

lua_iscfunction

```
int lua_iscfunction (lua_State *L, int index);
```

Returns 1 if the value at the given acceptable index is a C function, and 0 otherwise.

lua_isfunction

```
int lua_isfunction (lua_State *L, int index);
```

Returns 1 if the value at the given acceptable index is a function (either C or Lua), and 0 otherwise.

lua_islightuserdata

```
int lua_islightuserdata (lua_State *L, int index);
```

Returns 1 if the value at the given acceptable index is a light userdata, and 0 otherwise.

lua_isnil

```
int lua_isnil (lua_State *L, int index);
```

Returns 1 if the value at the given acceptable index is **nil**, and 0 otherwise.

lua_isnumber

```
int lua_isnumber (lua_State *L, int index);
```

Returns 1 if the value at the given acceptable index is a number or a string convertible to a number, and 0 otherwise.

lua_isstring

```
int lua_isstring (lua_State *L, int index);
```

Returns 1 if the value at the given acceptable index is a string or a number (which is always convertible to a string), and 0 otherwise.

lua_istable

```
int lua_istable (lua_State *L, int index);
```

Returns 1 if the value at the given acceptable index is a table, and 0 otherwise.

lua_isthread

```
int lua_isthread (lua_State *L, int index);
```

Returns 1 if the value at the given acceptable index is a thread, and 0 otherwise.

lua_isuserdata

```
int lua_isuserdata (lua_State *L, int index);
```

Returns 1 if the value at the given acceptable index is a userdata (either full or light), and 0 otherwise.

lua_lessthan

```
int lua_lessthan (lua_State *L, int index1, int index2);
```

Returns 1 if the value at acceptable index index1 is smaller than the value at acceptable index index2, following the semantics of the Lua < operator (that is, may call metamethods). Otherwise returns 0. Also returns 0 if any of the indices is non valid.

lua_load

```
int lua_load (lua_State *L,
              lua_Reader reader,
              void *data,
              const char *chunkname);
```

Loads a Lua chunk. If there are no errors, lua_load pushes the compiled chunk as a Lua function on top of the stack. Otherwise, it pushes an error message. The return values of lua_load are:

0: no errors;

LUA_ERRSYNTAX: syntax error during pre-compilation;

LUA_ERRMEM: memory allocation error.

This function only loads a chunk; it does not run it.

lua_load automatically detects whether the chunk is text or binary, and loads it accordingly (see program luac).

The lua_load function uses a user-supplied reader function to read the chunk (see lua_Reader on page 44). The data argument is an opaque value passed to the reader function.

The chunkname argument gives a name to the chunk, which is used for error messages and in debug information (see §3.8).

lua_newstate

```
lua_State *lua_newstate (lua_Alloc f, void *ud);
```

Creates a new, independent state. Returns NULL if cannot create the state (due to lack of memory). The argument f is the allocator function; Lua does all memory allocation for this state through this function. The second argument, ud, is an opaque pointer that Lua simply passes to the allocator in every call.

lua_newtable

```
void lua_newtable (lua_State *L);
```

Creates a new empty table and pushes it onto the stack. It is equivalent to lua_createtable(L, 0, 0).

lua_newthread

```
lua_State *lua_newthread (lua_State *L);
```

Creates a new thread, pushes it on the stack, and returns a pointer to a lua_State that represents this new thread. The new state returned by this function shares with the original state all global objects (such as tables), but has an independent execution stack.

There is no explicit function to close or to destroy a thread. Threads are subject to garbage collection, like any Lua object.

lua_newuserdata

```
void *lua_newuserdata (lua_State *L, size_t size);
```

This function allocates a new block of memory with the given size, pushes onto
the stack a new full userdata with the block address, and returns this address.

Userdata represents C values in Lua. A *full userdata* represents a block of
memory. It is an object (like a table): you must create it, it can have its own
metatable, and you can detect when it is being collected. A full userdata is only
equal to itself (under raw equality).

When Lua collects a full userdata with a gc metamethod, Lua calls the metamethod and marks the userdata as finalized. When this userdata is collected
again then Lua frees its corresponding memory.

lua_next

```
int lua_next (lua_State *L, int index);
```

Pops a key from the stack, and pushes a key-value pair from the table at the
given index (the "next" pair after the given key). If there are no more elements
in the table, then lua_next returns 0 (and pushes nothing).

A typical traversal looks like this:

```
/* table is in the stack at index 't' */
lua_pushnil(L);  /* first key */
while (lua_next(L, t) != 0) {
  /* uses 'key' (at index -2) and 'value' (at index -1) */
  printf("%s - %s\n",
         lua_typename(L, lua_type(L, -2)),
         lua_typename(L, lua_type(L, -1)));
  /* removes 'value'; keeps 'key' for next iteration */
  lua_pop(L, 1);
}
```

While traversing a table, do not call lua_tolstring directly on a key, unless
you know that the key is actually a string. Recall that lua_tolstring *changes*
the value at the given index; this confuses the next call to lua_next.

lua_Number

```
typedef double lua_Number;
```

The type of numbers in Lua. By default, it is double, but that can be changed in
luaconf.h.

Through the configuration file you can change Lua to operate with another
type for numbers (e.g., float or long).

lua_objlen

```
size_t lua_objlen (lua_State *L, int index);
```

Returns the "length" of the value at the given acceptable index: for strings, this is the string length; for tables, this is the result of the length operator ('#'); for userdata, this is the size of the block of memory allocated for the userdata; for other values, it is 0.

lua_pcall

```
lua_pcall (lua_State *L, int nargs, int nresults, int errfunc);
```

Calls a function in protected mode.

Both nargs and nresults have the same meaning as in lua_call. If there are no errors during the call, lua_pcall behaves exactly like lua_call. However, if there is any error, lua_pcall catches it, pushes a single value on the stack (the error message), and returns an error code. Like lua_call, lua_pcall always removes the function and its arguments from the stack.

If errfunc is 0, then the error message returned on the stack is exactly the original error message. Otherwise, errfunc is the stack index of an *error handler function*. (In the current implementation, this index cannot be a pseudo-index.) In case of runtime errors, this function will be called with the error message and its return value will be the message returned on the stack by lua_pcall.

Typically, the error handler function is used to add more debug information to the error message, such as a stack traceback. Such information cannot be gathered after the return of lua_pcall, since by then the stack has unwound.

The lua_pcall function returns 0 in case of success or one of the following error codes (defined in lua.h):

LUA_ERRRUN: a runtime error.

LUA_ERRMEM: memory allocation error. For such errors, Lua does not call the error handler function.

LUA_ERRERR: error while running the error handler function.

lua_pop

```
void lua_pop (lua_State *L, int n);
```

Pops n elements from the stack.

lua_pushboolean

```
void lua_pushboolean (lua_State *L, int b);
```

Pushes a boolean value with value b onto the stack.

lua_pushcclosure

```
void lua_pushcclosure (lua_State *L, lua_CFunction fn, int n);
```

Pushes a new C closure onto the stack.

When a C function is created, it is possible to associate some values with it, thus creating a C closure (see §3.4); these values are then accessible to the function whenever it is called. To associate values with a C function, first these values should be pushed onto the stack (when there are multiple values, the first value is pushed first). Then lua_pushcclosure is called to create and push the C function onto the stack, with the argument n telling how many values should be associated with the function. lua_pushcclosure also pops these values from the stack.

lua_pushcfunction

```
void lua_pushcfunction (lua_State *L, lua_CFunction f);
```

Pushes a C function onto the stack. This function receives a pointer to a C function and pushes onto the stack a Lua value of type function that, when called, invokes the corresponding C function.

Any function to be registered in Lua must follow the correct protocol to receive its parameters and return its results (see lua_CFunction on page 32).

lua_pushcfunction is defined as a macro:

```
#define lua_pushcfunction(L,f)  lua_pushcclosure(L,f,0)
```

lua_pushfstring

```
const char *lua_pushfstring (lua_State *L, const char *fmt, ...);
```

Pushes onto the stack a formatted string and returns a pointer to this string. It is similar to the C function sprintf, but has some important differences:

- You do not have to allocate space for the result: the result is a Lua string and Lua takes care of memory allocation (and deallocation, through garbage collection).

- The conversion specifiers are quite restricted. There are no flags, widths, or precisions. The conversion specifiers can only be '%%' (inserts a '%' in the string), '%s' (inserts a zero-terminated string, with no size restrictions), '%f' (inserts a lua_Number), '%p' (inserts a pointer as a hexadecimal numeral), '%d' (inserts an int), and '%c' (inserts an int as a character).

lua_pushinteger

```
void lua_pushinteger (lua_State *L, lua_Integer n);
```

Pushes a number with value n onto the stack.

lua_pushlightuserdata

```
void lua_pushlightuserdata (lua_State *L, void *p);
```

Pushes a light userdata onto the stack.

Userdata represents C values in Lua. A *light userdata* represents a pointer. It is a value (like a number): you do not create it, it has no individual metatable, and it is not collected (as it was never created). A light userdata is equal to "any" light userdata with the same C address.

lua_pushlstring

```
void lua_pushlstring (lua_State *L, const char *s, size_t len);
```

Pushes the string pointed to by s with size len onto the stack. Lua makes (or reuses) an internal copy of the given string, so the memory at s can be freed or reused immediately after the function returns. The string can contain embedded zeros.

lua_pushnil

```
void lua_pushnil (lua_State *L);
```

Pushes a nil value onto the stack.

lua_pushnumber

```
void lua_pushnumber (lua_State *L, lua_Number n);
```

Pushes a number with value n onto the stack.

lua_pushstring

```
void lua_pushstring (lua_State *L, const char *s);
```

Pushes the zero-terminated string pointed to by s onto the stack. Lua makes (or reuses) an internal copy of the given string, so the memory at s can be freed or reused immediately after the function returns. The string cannot contain embedded zeros; it is assumed to end at the first zero.

lua_pushthread

```
int lua_pushthread (lua_State *L);
```

Pushes the thread represented by L onto the stack. Returns 1 if this thread is the main thread of its state.

lua_pushvalue

```
void lua_pushvalue (lua_State *L, int index);
```

Pushes a copy of the element at the given valid index onto the stack.

lua_pushvfstring

```
const char *lua_pushvfstring (lua_State *L,
                              const char *fmt,
                              va_list argp);
```

Equivalent to lua_pushfstring, except that it receives a va_list instead of a variable number of arguments.

lua_rawequal

```
int lua_rawequal (lua_State *L, int index1, int index2);
```

Returns 1 if the two values in acceptable indices index1 and index2 are primitively equal (that is, without calling metamethods). Otherwise returns 0. Also returns 0 if any of the indices are non valid.

lua_rawget

```
void lua_rawget (lua_State *L, int index);
```

Similar to lua_gettable, but does a raw access (i.e., without metamethods).

lua_rawgeti

```
void lua_rawgeti (lua_State *L, int index, int n);
```

Pushes onto the stack the value t[n], where t is the value at the given valid index index. The access is raw; that is, it does not invoke metamethods.

lua_rawset

```
void lua_rawset (lua_State *L, int index);
```

Similar to lua_settable, but does a raw assignment (i.e., without metamethods).

lua_rawseti

```
void lua_rawseti (lua_State *L, int index, int n);
```

Does the equivalent of t[n]=v, where t is the value at the given valid index index and v is the value at the top of the stack,

This function pops the value from the stack. The assignment is raw; that is, it does not invoke metamethods.

lua_Reader

```
typedef const char * (*lua_Reader) (lua_State *L,
                                    void *data,
                                    size_t *size);
```

The reader function used by `lua_load`. Every time it needs another piece of the chunk, `lua_load` calls the reader, passing along its `data` parameter. The reader must return a pointer to a block of memory with a new piece of the chunk and set `size` to the block size. The block must exist until the reader function is called again. To signal the end of the chunk, the reader must return `NULL`. The reader function may return pieces of any size greater than zero.

lua_register

```
void lua_register (lua_State *L,
                   const char *name,
                   lua_CFunction f);
```

Sets the C function `f` as the new value of global `name`. It is defined as a macro:

```
#define lua_register(L,n,f) \
        (lua_pushcfunction(L, f), lua_setglobal(L, n))
```

lua_remove

```
void lua_remove (lua_State *L, int index);
```

Removes the element at the given valid index, shifting down the elements above this index to fill the gap. Cannot be called with a pseudo-index, because a pseudo-index is not an actual stack position.

lua_replace

```
void lua_replace (lua_State *L, int index);
```

Moves the top element into the given position (and pops it), without shifting any element (therefore replacing the value at the given position).

lua_resume

```
int lua_resume (lua_State *L, int narg);
```

Starts and resumes a coroutine in a given thread.

To start a coroutine, you first create a new thread (see `lua_newthread` on page 38); then you push onto its stack the main function plus any arguments; then you call `lua_resume`, with `narg` being the number of arguments. This call returns when the coroutine suspends or finishes its execution. When it returns, the stack contains all values passed to `lua_yield`, or all values returned by the body function. `lua_resume` returns `LUA_YIELD` if the coroutine yields, 0 if the coroutine finishes its execution without errors, or an error code in case of errors (see lua_pcall on page 40). In case of errors, the stack is not unwound, so you can use the debug API over it. The error message is on the top of the stack. To restart a coroutine, you put on its stack only the values to be passed as results from yield, and then call lua_resume.

lua_setallocf

```
void lua_setallocf (lua_State *L, lua_Alloc f, void *ud);
```

Changes the allocator function of a given state to f with user data ud.

lua_setfenv

```
int lua_setfenv (lua_State *L, int index);
```

Pops a table from the stack and sets it as the new environment for the value at the given index. If the value at the given index is neither a function nor a thread nor a userdata, lua_setfenv returns 0. Otherwise it returns 1.

lua_setfield

```
void lua_setfield (lua_State *L, int index, const char *k);
```

Does the equivalent to t[k]=v, where t is the value at the given valid index index and v is the value at the top of the stack,

This function pops the value from the stack. As in Lua, this function may trigger a metamethod for the "newindex" event (see §2.8).

lua_setglobal

```
void lua_setglobal (lua_State *L, const char *name);
```

Pops a value from the stack and sets it as the new value of global name. It is defined as a macro:

```
#define lua_setglobal(L,s)   lua_setfield(L, LUA_GLOBALSINDEX, s)
```

lua_setmetatable

```
int lua_setmetatable (lua_State *L, int index);
```

Pops a table from the stack and sets it as the new metatable for the value at the given acceptable index.

lua_settable

```
void lua_settable (lua_State *L, int index);
```

Does the equivalent to `t[k]=v`, where `t` is the value at the given valid index `index`, `v` is the value at the top of the stack, and `k` is the value just below the top.

This function pops both the key and the value from the stack. As in Lua, this function may trigger a metamethod for the "newindex" event (see §2.8).

lua_settop

```
void lua_settop (lua_State *L, int index);
```

Accepts any acceptable index, or 0, and sets the stack top to this index. If the new top is larger than the old one, then the new elements are filled with **nil**. If `index` is 0, then all stack elements are removed.

lua_State

```
typedef struct lua_State lua_State;
```

Opaque structure that keeps the whole state of a Lua interpreter. The Lua library is fully reentrant: it has no global variables. All information about a state is kept in this structure.

A pointer to this state must be passed as the first argument to every function in the library, except to `lua_newstate`, which creates a Lua state from scratch.

lua_status

```
int lua_status (lua_State *L);
```

Returns the status of the thread L.

The status can be 0 for a normal thread, an error code if the thread finished its execution with an error, or `LUA_YIELD` if the thread is suspended.

lua_toboolean

```
int lua_toboolean (lua_State *L, int index);
```

Converts the Lua value at the given acceptable index to a C boolean value (0 or 1). Like all tests in Lua, `lua_toboolean` returns 1 for any Lua value different from **false** and **nil**; otherwise it returns 0. It also returns 0 when called with a non-valid index. (If you want to accept only actual boolean values, use `lua_isboolean` to test the value's type.)

lua_tocfunction

```
lua_CFunction lua_tocfunction (lua_State *L, int index);
```

Converts a value at the given acceptable index to a C function. That value must be a C function; otherwise, returns `NULL`.

lua_tointeger

```
lua_Integer lua_tointeger (lua_State *L, int idx);
```

Converts the Lua value at the given acceptable index to the signed integral type lua_Integer. The Lua value must be a number or a string convertible to a number (see §2.2.1); otherwise, lua_tointeger returns 0.

If the number is not an integer, it is truncated in some non-specified way.

lua_tolstring

```
const char *lua_tolstring (lua_State *L, int index, size_t *len);
```

Converts the Lua value at the given acceptable index to a C string. If len is not NULL, it also sets *len with the string length. The Lua value must be a string or a number; otherwise, the function returns NULL. If the value is a number, then lua_tolstring also *changes the actual value in the stack to a string*. (This change confuses lua_next when lua_tolstring is applied to keys during a table traversal.)

lua_tolstring returns a fully aligned pointer to a string inside the Lua state. This string always has a zero ('\0') after its last character (as in C), but may contain other zeros in its body. Because Lua has garbage collection, there is no guarantee that the pointer returned by lua_tolstring will be valid after the corresponding value is removed from the stack.

lua_tonumber

```
lua_Number lua_tonumber (lua_State *L, int index);
```

Converts the Lua value at the given acceptable index to the C type lua_Number (see lua_Number on page 39). The Lua value must be a number or a string convertible to a number (see §2.2.1); otherwise, lua_tonumber returns 0.

lua_topointer

```
const void *lua_topointer (lua_State *L, int index);
```

Converts the value at the given acceptable index to a generic C pointer (void*). The value may be a userdata, a table, a thread, or a function; otherwise, lua_topointer returns NULL. Different objects will give different pointers. There is no way to convert the pointer back to its original value.

Typically this function is used only for debug information.

lua_tostring

```
const char *lua_tostring (lua_State *L, int index);
```

Equivalent to lua_tolstring with len equal to NULL.

lua_tothread

```
lua_State *lua_tothread (lua_State *L, int index);
```

Converts the value at the given acceptable index to a Lua thread (represented as lua_State*). This value must be a thread; otherwise, the function returns NULL.

lua_touserdata

```
void *lua_touserdata (lua_State *L, int index);
```

If the value at the given acceptable index is a full userdata, returns its block address. If the value is a light userdata, returns its pointer. Otherwise, returns NULL.

lua_type

```
int lua_type (lua_State *L, int index);
```

Returns the type of the value in the given acceptable index, or LUA_TNONE for a non-valid index (that is, an index to an "empty" stack position). The types returned by lua_type are coded by the following constants defined in lua.h: LUA_TNIL, LUA_TNUMBER, LUA_TBOOLEAN, LUA_TSTRING, LUA_TTABLE, LUA_TFUNCTION, LUA_TUSERDATA, LUA_TTHREAD, and LUA_TLIGHTUSERDATA.

lua_typename

```
const char *lua_typename  (lua_State *L, int tp);
```

Returns the name of the type encoded by the value tp, which must be one the values returned by lua_type.

lua_Writer

```
typedef int (*lua_Writer) (lua_State *L,
                           const void* p,
                           size_t sz,
                           void* ud);
```

The writer function used by lua_dump. Every time it produces another piece of chunk, lua_dump calls the writer, passing along the buffer to be written (p), its size (sz), and the data parameter supplied to lua_dump.

The writer returns an error code: 0 means no errors; any other value means an error and stops lua_dump from calling the writer again.

lua_xmove

```
void lua_xmove (lua_State *from, lua_State *to, int n);
```

Exchange values between different threads of the *same* global state.

This function pops n values from the stack from, and pushes them onto the stack to.

lua_yield

```
int lua_yield (lua_State *L, int nresults);
```

Yields a coroutine.

This function should only be called as the return expression of a C function, as follows:

```
return lua_yield (L, nresults);
```

When a C function calls lua_yield in that way, the running coroutine suspends its execution, and the call to lua_resume that started this coroutine returns. The parameter nresults is the number of values from the stack that are passed as results to lua_resume.

3.8   The Debug Interface

Lua has no built-in debugging facilities. Instead, it offers a special interface by means of functions and *hooks*. This interface allows the construction of different kinds of debuggers, profilers, and other tools that need "inside information" from the interpreter.

lua_Debug

```
typedef struct lua_Debug {
  int event;
  const char *name;         /* (n) */
  const char *namewhat;     /* (n) */
  const char *what;         /* (S) */
  const char *source;       /* (S) */
  int currentline;          /* (l) */
  int nups;                 /* (u) number of upvalues */
  int linedefined;          /* (S) */
  int lastlinedefined;      /* (S) */
  char short_src[LUA_IDSIZE]; /* (S) */
  /* private part */
  other fields
} lua_Debug;
```

A structure used to carry different pieces of information about an active function. `lua_getstack` fills only the private part of this structure, for later use. To fill the other fields of `lua_Debug` with useful information, call `lua_getinfo`.

The fields of `lua_Debug` have the following meaning:

source: If the function was defined in a string, then `source` is that string. If the function was defined in a file, then `source` starts with a '`@`' followed by the file name.

short_src: a "printable" version of `source`, to be used in error messages.

linedefined: the line number where the definition of the function starts.

lastlinedefined: the line number where the definition of the function ends.

what: the string `"Lua"` if the function is a Lua function, `"C"` if it is a C function, `"main"` if it is the main part of a chunk, and `"tail"` if it was a function that did a tail call. In the latter case, Lua has no other information about the function.

currentline: the current line where the given function is executing. When no line information is available, `currentline` is set to –1.

name: a reasonable name for the given function. Because functions in Lua are first-class values, they do not have a fixed name: some functions may be the value of multiple global variables, while others may be stored only in a table field. The `lua_getinfo` function checks how the function was called to find a suitable name. If it cannot find a name, then `name` is set to NULL.

namewhat: explains the `name` field. The value of `namewhat` can be `"global"`, `"local"`, `"method"`, `"field"`, `"upvalue"`, or `""` (the empty string), according to how the function was called. (Lua uses the empty string when no other option seems to apply.)

nups: the number of upvalues of the function.

lua_gethook

```
lua_Hook lua_gethook (lua_State *L);
```

Returns the current hook function.

lua_gethookcount

```
int lua_gethookcount (lua_State *L);
```

Returns the current hook count.

lua_gethookmask

```
int lua_gethookmask (lua_State *L);
```

Returns the current hook mask.

lua_getinfo

```
int lua_getinfo (lua_State *L, const char *what, lua_Debug *ar);
```

Returns information about a specific function or function invocation.

To get information about a function invocation, the parameter ar must be a valid activation record that was filled by a previous call to lua_getstack or given as argument to a hook (see lua_Hook on page 52).

To get information about a function you push it onto the stack and start the what string with the character '>'. (In that case, lua_getinfo pops the function in the top of the stack.) For instance, to know in which line a function f was defined, you can write the following code:

```
lua_Debug ar;
lua_getfield(L, LUA_GLOBALSINDEX, "f");  /* get global 'f' */
lua_getinfo(L, ">S", &ar);
printf("%d\n", ar.linedefined);
```

Each character in the string what selects some fields of the structure ar to be filled or a value to be pushed on the stack:

'n': fills in the field name and namewhat;

'S': fills in the fields source, short_src, linedefined, lastlinedefined, and what;

'l': fills in the field currentline;

'u': fills in the field nups;

'f': pushes onto the stack the function that is running at the given level;

'L': pushes onto the stack a table whose indices are the numbers of the lines that are valid on the function. (A *valid line* is a line with some associated code, that is, a line where you can put a break point. Non-valid lines include empty lines and comments.)

This function returns 0 on error (for instance, an invalid option in what).

lua_getlocal

```
const char *lua_getlocal (lua_State *L, lua_Debug *ar, int n);
```

Gets information about a local variable of a given activation record. The parameter ar must be a valid activation record that was filled by a previous call to lua_getstack or given as argument to a hook (see lua_Hook on page 52). The index n selects which local variable to inspect (1 is the first parameter or active local variable, and so on, until the last active local variable). lua_getlocal pushes the variable's value onto the stack and returns its name.

Variable names starting with '(' (open parentheses) represent internal variables (loop control variables, temporaries, and C function locals).

Returns NULL (and pushes nothing) when the index is greater than the number of active local variables.

lua_getstack

```
int lua_getstack (lua_State *L, int level, lua_Debug *ar);
```

Get information about the interpreter runtime stack.

This function fills parts of a lua_Debug structure with an identification of the *activation record* of the function executing at a given level. Level 0 is the current running function, whereas level $n + 1$ is the function that has called level n. When there are no errors, lua_getstack returns 1; when called with a level greater than the stack depth, it returns 0.

lua_getupvalue

```
const char *lua_getupvalue (lua_State *L, int funcindex, int n);
```

Gets information about a closure's upvalue. (For Lua functions, upvalues are the external local variables that the function uses, and that are consequently included in its closure.) lua_getupvalue gets the index n of an upvalue, pushes the upvalue's value onto the stack, and returns its name. funcindex points to the closure in the stack. (Upvalues have no particular order, as they are active through the whole function. So, they are numbered in an arbitrary order.)

Returns NULL (and pushes nothing) when the index is greater than the number of upvalues. For C functions, this function uses the empty string "" as a name for all upvalues.

lua_Hook

```
typedef void (*lua_Hook) (lua_State *L, lua_Debug *ar);
```

Type for debugging hook functions.

Whenever a hook is called, its ar argument has its field event set to the specific event that triggered the hook. Lua identifies these events with the following constants: LUA_HOOKCALL, LUA_HOOKRET, LUA_HOOKTAILRET, LUA_HOOKLINE, and LUA_HOOKCOUNT. Moreover, for line events, the field currentline is also set. To get the value of any other field in ar, the hook must call lua_getinfo. For return events, event may be LUA_HOOKRET, the normal value, or LUA_HOOKTAILRET.

In the latter case, Lua is simulating a return from a function that did a tail call; in this case, it is useless to call lua_getinfo.

While Lua is running a hook, it disables other calls to hooks. Therefore, if a hook calls back Lua to execute a function or a chunk, this execution occurs without any calls to hooks.

lua_sethook

```
int lua_sethook (lua_State *L, lua_Hook f, int mask, int count);
```

Sets the debugging hook function.

Argument f is the hook function. mask specifies on which events the hook will be called: it is formed by a bitwise or of the constants LUA_MASKCALL, LUA_MASKRET, LUA_MASKLINE, and LUA_MASKCOUNT. The count argument is only meaningful when the mask includes LUA_MASKCOUNT. For each event, the hook is called as explained below:

The call hook: is called when the interpreter calls a function. The hook is called just after Lua enters the new function, before the function gets its arguments.

The return hook: is called when the interpreter returns from a function. The hook is called just before Lua leaves the function. You have no access to the values to be returned by the function.

The line hook: is called when the interpreter is about to start the execution of a new line of code, or when it jumps back in the code (even to the same line). (This event only happens while Lua is executing a Lua function.)

The count hook: is called after the interpreter executes every count instructions. (This event only happens while Lua is executing a Lua function.)

A hook is disabled by setting mask to zero.

lua_setlocal

```
const char *lua_setlocal (lua_State *L, lua_Debug *ar, int n);
```

Sets the value of a local variable of a given activation record. Parameters ar and n are as in lua_getlocal (see lua_getlocal on page 51). lua_setlocal assigns the value at the top of the stack to the variable and returns its name. It also pops the value from the stack.

Returns NULL (and pops nothing) when the index is greater than the number of active local variables.

lua_setupvalue

```
const char *lua_setupvalue (lua_State *L, int funcindex, int n);
```

Sets the value of a closure's upvalue. It assigns the value at the top of the stack to the upvalue and returns its name. It also pops the value from the stack. Parameters funcindex and n are as in the lua_getupvalue (see lua_getupvalue on page 52).

Returns NULL (and pops nothing) when the index is greater than the number of upvalues.

4 The Auxiliary Library

The *auxiliary library* provides several convenient functions to interface C with
Lua. While the basic API provides the primitive functions for all interactions
between C and Lua, the auxiliary library provides higher-level functions for
some common tasks.

All functions from the auxiliary library are defined in header file lauxlib.h
and have a prefix luaL_.

All functions in the auxiliary library are built on top of the basic API, and so
they provide nothing that cannot be done with this API.

Several functions in the auxiliary library are used to check C function arguments. Their names are always luaL_check* or luaL_opt*. All of these functions
raise an error if the check is not satisfied. Because the error message is formatted for arguments (e.g., "bad argument #1"), you should not use these functions
for other stack values.

4.1 Functions and Types

Here we list all functions and types from the auxiliary library in alphabetical
order.

luaL_addchar

```
void luaL_addchar (luaL_Buffer *B, char c);
```

Adds the character c to the buffer B (see luaL_Buffer on page 56).

luaL_addlstring

```
void luaL_addlstring (luaL_Buffer *B, const char *s, size_t l);
```

Adds the string pointed to by s with length l to the buffer B (see luaL_Buffer on
page 56). The string may contain embedded zeros.

luaL_addsize

```
void luaL_addsize (luaL_Buffer *B, size_t n);
```

Adds to the buffer B (see luaL_Buffer on page 56) a string of length n previously
copied to the buffer area (see luaL_prepbuffer on page 62).

luaL_addstring

```
void luaL_addstring (luaL_Buffer *B, const char *s);
```

Adds the zero-terminated string pointed to by s to the buffer B (see luaL_Buffer
on page 56). The string may not contain embedded zeros.

luaL_addvalue

```
void luaL_addvalue (luaL_Buffer *B);
```

Adds the value at the top of the stack to the buffer B (see `luaL_Buffer` on page 56). Pops the value.

This is the only function on string buffers that can (and must) be called with an extra element on the stack, which is the value to be added to the buffer.

luaL_argcheck

```
void luaL_argcheck (lua_State *L,
                    int cond,
                    int narg,
                    const char *extramsg);
```

Checks whether `cond` is true. If not, raises an error with the following message, where `func` is retrieved from the call stack:

```
bad argument #<narg> to <func> (<extramsg>)
```

luaL_argerror

```
int luaL_argerror (lua_State *L, int narg, const char *extramsg);
```

Raises an error with the following message, where `func` is retrieved from the call stack:

```
bad argument #<narg> to <func> (<extramsg>)
```

This function never returns, but it is an idiom to use it in C functions as return `luaL_argerror`(*args*).

luaL_Buffer

```
typedef struct luaL_Buffer luaL_Buffer;
```

Type for a *string buffer*.

A string buffer allows C code to build Lua strings piecemeal. Its pattern of use is as follows:

- First you declare a variable b of type `luaL_Buffer`.

- Then you initialize it with a call `luaL_buffinit`(L, &b).

- Then you add string pieces to the buffer calling any of the `luaL_add*` functions.

- You finish by calling `luaL_pushresult`(&b). This call leaves the final string on the top of the stack.

During its normal operation, a string buffer uses a variable number of stack slots. So, while using a buffer, you cannot assume that you know where the top of the stack is. You can use the stack between successive calls to buffer operations as long as that use is balanced; that is, when you call a buffer operation, the stack is at the same level it was immediately after the previous buffer operation. (The only exception to this rule is luaL_addvalue.) After calling luaL_pushresult the stack is back to its level when the buffer was initialized, plus the final string on its top.

luaL_buffinit

```
void luaL_buffinit (lua_State *L, luaL_Buffer *B);
```

Initializes a buffer B. This function does not allocate any space; the buffer must be declared as a variable (see luaL_Buffer on page 56).

luaL_callmeta

```
int luaL_callmeta (lua_State *L, int obj, const char *e);
```

Calls a metamethod.

If the object at index obj has a metatable and this metatable has a field e, this function calls this field and passes the object as its only argument. In this case this function returns 1 and pushes onto the stack the value returned by the call. If there is no metatable or no metamethod, this function returns 0 (without pushing any value on the stack).

luaL_checkany

```
void luaL_checkany (lua_State *L, int narg);
```

Checks whether the function has an argument of any type (including **nil**) at position narg.

luaL_checkint

```
int luaL_checkint (lua_State *L, int narg);
```

Checks whether the function argument narg is a number and returns this number cast to an int.

luaL_checkinteger

```
lua_Integer luaL_checkinteger (lua_State *L, int narg);
```

Checks whether the function argument narg is a number and returns this number cast to a lua_Integer.

luaL_checklong

```
long luaL_checklong (lua_State *L, int narg);
```

Checks whether the function argument narg is a number and returns this number cast to a long.

luaL_checklstring

```
const char *luaL_checklstring (lua_State *L, int narg, size_t *l);
```

Checks whether the function argument narg is a string and returns this string; if l is not NULL fills *l with the string's length.

luaL_checknumber

```
lua_Number luaL_checknumber (lua_State *L, int narg);
```

Checks whether the function argument narg is a number and returns this number.

luaL_checkoption

```
int luaL_checkoption (lua_State *L,
                      int narg,
                      const char *def,
                      const char *const lst[]);
```

Checks whether the function argument narg is a string and searches for this string in the array lst (which must be NULL-terminated). Returns the index in the array where the string was found. Raises an error if the argument is not a string or if the string cannot be found.

If def is not NULL, the function uses def as a default value when there is no argument narg or if this argument is **nil**.

This is a useful function for mapping strings to C enums. (The usual convention in Lua libraries is to use strings instead of numbers to select options.)

luaL_checkstack

```
void luaL_checkstack (lua_State *L, int sz, const char *msg);
```

Grows the stack size to top+sz elements, raising an error if the stack cannot grow to that size. msg is an additional text to go into the error message.

luaL_checkstring

```
const char *luaL_checkstring (lua_State *L, int narg);
```

Checks whether the function argument narg is a string and returns this string.

luaL_checktype

```
void luaL_checktype (lua_State *L, int narg, int t);
```

Checks whether the function argument narg has type t.

luaL_checkudata

```
void *luaL_checkudata (lua_State *L, int narg, const char *tname);
```

Checks whether the function argument narg is a userdata of the type tname (see luaL_newmetatable on page 61).

luaL_dofile

```
int luaL_dofile (lua_State *L, const char *filename);
```

Loads and runs the given file. It is defined as the following macro:

```
(luaL_loadfile(L, filename) || lua_pcall(L, 0, LUA_MULTRET, 0))
```

It returns 0 if there are no errors or 1 in case of errors.

luaL_dostring

```
int luaL_dostring (lua_State *L, const char *str);
```

Loads and runs the given string. It is defined as the following macro:

```
(luaL_loadstring(L, str) || lua_pcall(L, 0, LUA_MULTRET, 0))
```

It returns 0 if there are no errors or 1 in case of errors.

luaL_error

```
int luaL_error (lua_State *L, const char *fmt, ...);
```

Raises an error. The error message format is given by fmt plus any extra arguments, following the same rules of lua_pushfstring. It also adds at the beginning of the message the file name and the line number where the error occurred, if this information is available.

This function never returns, but it is an idiom to use it in C functions as return luaL_error(*args*).

luaL_getmetafield

```
int luaL_getmetafield (lua_State *L, int obj, const char *e);
```

Pushes onto the stack the field e from the metatable of the object at index obj. If the object does not have a metatable, or if the metatable does not have this field, returns 0 and pushes nothing.

luaL_getmetatable

```
void luaL_getmetatable (lua_State *L, const char *tname);
```

Pushes onto the stack the metatable associated with name tname in the registry (see luaL_newmetatable on page 61).

luaL_gsub

```
const char *luaL_gsub (lua_State *L,
                       const char *s,
                       const char *p,
                       const char *r);
```

Creates a copy of string s by replacing any occurrence of the string p with the string r. Pushes the resulting string on the stack and returns it.

luaL_loadbuffer

```
int luaL_loadbuffer (lua_State *L,
                     const char *buff,
                     size_t sz,
                     const char *name);
```

Loads a buffer as a Lua chunk. This function uses lua_load to load the chunk in the buffer pointed to by buff with size sz.

This function returns the same results as lua_load. name is the chunk name, used for debug information and error messages.

luaL_loadfile

```
int luaL_loadfile (lua_State *L, const char *filename);
```

Loads a file as a Lua chunk. This function uses lua_load to load the chunk in the file named filename. If filename is NULL, then it loads from the standard input. The first line in the file is ignored if it starts with a #.

This function returns the same results as lua_load, but it has an extra error code LUA_ERRFILE if it cannot open/read the file.

As lua_load, this function only loads the chunk; it does not run it.

luaL_loadstring

```
int luaL_loadstring (lua_State *L, const char *s);
```

Loads a string as a Lua chunk. This function uses lua_load to load the chunk in the zero-terminated string s.

This function returns the same results as lua_load.

Also as lua_load, this function only loads the chunk; it does not run it.

luaL_newmetatable

```
int luaL_newmetatable (lua_State *L, const char *tname);
```

If the registry already has the key tname, returns 0. Otherwise, creates a new table to be used as a metatable for userdata, adds it to the registry with key tname, and returns 1.

In both cases pushes onto the stack the final value associated with tname in the registry.

luaL_newstate

```
lua_State *luaL_newstate (void);
```

Creates a new Lua state. It calls lua_newstate with an allocator based on the standard C realloc function and then sets a panic function (see lua_atpanic on page 31) that prints an error message to the standard error output in case of fatal errors.

Returns the new state, or NULL if there is a memory allocation error.

luaL_openlibs

```
void luaL_openlibs (lua_State *L);
```

Opens all standard Lua libraries into the given state.

luaL_optint

```
int luaL_optint (lua_State *L, int narg, int d);
```

If the function argument narg is a number, returns this number cast to an int. If this argument is absent or is **nil**, returns d. Otherwise, raises an error.

luaL_optinteger

```
lua_Integer luaL_optinteger (lua_State *L,
                             int narg,
                             lua_Integer d);
```

If the function argument narg is a number, returns this number cast to a lua_Integer. If this argument is absent or is **nil**, returns d. Otherwise, raises an error.

luaL_optlong

```
long luaL_optlong (lua_State *L, int narg, long d);
```

If the function argument narg is a number, returns this number cast to a long. If this argument is absent or is **nil**, returns d. Otherwise, raises an error.

luaL_optlstring

```
const char *luaL_optlstring (lua_State *L,
                             int narg,
                             const char *d,
                             size_t *l);
```

If the function argument narg is a string, returns this string. If this argument is absent or is **nil**, returns d. Otherwise, raises an error.

If l is not NULL, fills the position *l with the results's length.

luaL_optnumber

```
lua_Number luaL_optnumber (lua_State *L, int narg, lua_Number d);
```

If the function argument narg is a number, returns this number. If this argument is absent or is **nil**, returns d. Otherwise, raises an error.

luaL_optstring

```
const char *luaL_optstring (lua_State *L,
                            int narg,
                            const char *d);
```

If the function argument narg is a string, returns this string. If this argument is absent or is **nil**, returns d. Otherwise, raises an error.

luaL_prepbuffer

```
char *luaL_prepbuffer (luaL_Buffer *B);
```

Returns an address to a space of size LUAL_BUFFERSIZE where you can copy a string to be added to buffer B (see luaL_Buffer on page 56). After copying the string into this space you must call luaL_addsize with the size of the string to actually add it to the buffer.

luaL_pushresult

```
void luaL_pushresult (luaL_Buffer *B);
```

Finishes the use of buffer B leaving the final string on the top of the stack.

luaL_ref

```
int luaL_ref (lua_State *L, int t);
```

Creates and returns a *reference*, in the table at index t, for the object at the top of the stack (and pops the object).

A reference is a unique integer key. As long as you do not manually add integer keys into table t, luaL_ref ensures the uniqueness of the key it returns. You can retrieve an object referred by reference r by calling lua_rawgeti(L, t, r). Function luaL_unref frees a reference and its associated object.

If the object at the top of the stack is **nil**, luaL_ref returns the constant LUA_REFNIL. The constant LUA_NOREF is guaranteed to be different from any reference returned by luaL_ref.

luaL_Reg

```
typedef struct luaL_Reg {
  const char *name;
  lua_CFunction func;
} luaL_Reg;
```

Type for arrays of functions to be registered by luaL_register. name is the function name and func is a pointer to the function. Any array of luaL_Reg must end with an sentinel entry in which both name and func are NULL.

luaL_register

```
void luaL_register (lua_State *L,
                    const char *libname,
                    const luaL_Reg *l);
```

Opens a library.

When called with libname equal to NULL, it simply registers all functions in the list l (see luaL_Reg on page 63) into the table on the top of the stack.

When called with a non-null libname, luaL_register creates a new table t, sets it as the value of the global variable libname, sets it as the value of package.loaded[libname], and registers on it all functions in the list l. If there is a table in package.loaded[libname] or in variable libname, reuses this table instead of creating a new one.

In any case the function leaves the table on the top of the stack.

luaL_typename

```
const char *luaL_typename (lua_State *L, int idx);
```

Returns the name of the type of the value at index idx.

luaL_typerror

```
int luaL_typerror (lua_State *L, int narg, const char *tname);
```

Generates an error with a message like the following:

location: bad argument *narg* to 'func' (*tname* expected, got *rt*)

where *location* is produced by luaL_where, *func* is the name of the current function, and *rt* is the type name of the actual argument.

luaL_unref

```
void luaL_unref (lua_State *L, int t, int ref);
```

Releases reference ref from the table at index t (see luaL_ref on page 62). The entry is removed from the table, so that the referred object can be collected. The reference ref is also freed to be used again.

If ref is LUA_NOREF or LUA_REFNIL, luaL_unref does nothing.

luaL_where

```
void luaL_where (lua_State *L, int lvl);
```

Pushes onto the stack a string identifying the current position of the control at level lvl in the call stack. Typically this string has the following format:

chunkname:*currentline*:

Level 0 is the running function, level 1 is the function that called the running function, etc.

This function is used to build a prefix for error messages.

5 Standard Libraries

The standard Lua libraries provide useful functions that are implemented directly through the C API. Some of these functions provide essential services to the language (e.g., `type` and `getmetatable`); others provide access to "outside" services (e.g., I/O); and others could be implemented in Lua itself, but are quite useful or have critical performance requirements that deserve an implementation in C (e.g., `sort`).

All libraries are implemented through the official C API and are provided as separate C modules. Currently, Lua has the following standard libraries:

- basic library;

- package library;

- string manipulation;

- table manipulation;

- mathematical functions (sin, log, etc.);

- input and output;

- operating system facilities;

- debug facilities.

Except for the basic and package libraries, each library provides all its functions as fields of a global table or as methods of its objects.

To have access to these libraries, the C host program should call the `luaL_openlibs` function, which opens all standard libraries. Alternatively, it can open them individually by calling `luaopen_base` (for the basic library), `luaopen_package` (for the package library), `luaopen_string` (for the string library), `luaopen_table` (for the table library), `luaopen_math` (for the mathematical library), `luaopen_io` (for the I/O and the Operating System libraries), and `luaopen_debug` (for the debug library). These functions are declared in `lualib.h` and should not be called directly: you must call them like any other Lua C function, e.g., by using `lua_call`.

5.1 Basic Functions

The basic library provides some core functions to Lua. If you do not include this library in your application, you should check carefully whether you need to provide implementations for some of its facilities.

assert (v [, message])

Issues an error when the value of its argument v is false (i.e., **nil** or **false**); otherwise, returns all its arguments. message is an error message; when absent, it defaults to "assertion failed!"

collectgarbage (opt [, arg])

This function is a generic interface to the garbage collector. It performs different functions according to its first argument, opt:

"stop": stops the garbage collector.

"restart": restarts the garbage collector.

"collect": performs a full garbage-collection cycle.

"count": returns the total memory in use by Lua (in Kbytes).

"step": performs a garbage-collection step. The step "size" is controlled by arg (larger values mean more steps) in a non-specified way. If you want to control the step size you must experimentally tune the value of arg. Returns **true** if the step finished a collection cycle.

"setpause": sets arg/100 as the new value for the *pause* of the collector (see §2.10).

"setstepmul": sets arg/100 as the new value for the *step multiplier* of the collector (see §2.10).

dofile (filename)

Opens the named file and executes its contents as a Lua chunk. When called without arguments, dofile executes the contents of the standard input (stdin). Returns all values returned by the chunk. In case of errors, dofile propagates the error to its caller (that is, dofile does not run in protected mode).

error (message [, level])

Terminates the last protected function called and returns message as the error message. Function error never returns.

Usually, error adds some information about the error position at the beginning of the message. The level argument specifies how to get the error position. With level 1 (the default), the error position is where the error function was called. Level 2 points the error to where the function that called error was called; and so on. Passing a level 0 avoids the addition of error position information to the message.

_G

A global variable (not a function) that holds the global environment (that is, _G._G=_G). Lua itself does not use this variable; changing its value does not affect any environment, nor vice-versa. (Use setfenv to change environments.)

getfenv (f)

Returns the current environment in use by the function. f can be a Lua function or a number that specifies the function at that stack level: Level 1 is the function calling getfenv. If the given function is not a Lua function, or if f is 0, getfenv returns the global environment. The default for f is 1.

getmetatable (object)

If object does not have a metatable, returns **nil**. Otherwise, if the object's metatable has a "__metatable" field, returns the associated value. Otherwise, returns the metatable of the given object.

ipairs (t)

Returns three values: an iterator function, the table t, and 0, so that the construction

```
for i,v in ipairs(t) do body end
```

will iterate over the pairs (1,t[1]), (2,t[2]), ···, up to the first integer key absent from the table.

load (func [, chunkname])

Loads a chunk using function func to get its pieces. Each call to func must return a string that concatenates with previous results. A return of **nil** (or no value) signals the end of the chunk.

If there are no errors, returns the compiled chunk as a function; otherwise, returns **nil** plus the error message. The environment of the returned function is the global environment.

chunkname is used as the chunk name for error messages and debug information.

loadfile ([filename])

Similar to load, but gets the chunk from file filename or from the standard input, if no file name is given.

loadstring (string [, chunkname])

Similar to load, but gets the chunk from the given string.

To load and run a given string, use the idiom

```
assert(loadstring(s))()
```

next (table [, index])

Allows a program to traverse all fields of a table. Its first argument is a table and its second argument is an index in this table. next returns the next index of the table and its associated value. When called with **nil** as its second argument, next returns an initial index and its associated value. When called with the last index, or with **nil** in an empty table, next returns **nil**. If the second argument is absent, then it is interpreted as **nil**. In particular, you can use next(t) to check whether a table is empty.

The order in which the indices are enumerated is not specified, *even for numeric indices*. (To traverse a table in numeric order, use a numerical **for** or the ipairs function.)

The behavior of next is *undefined* if, during the traversal, you assign any value to a non-existent field in the table. You may however modify existing fields. In particular, you may clear existing fields.

pairs (t)

Returns three values: the next function, the table t, and **nil**, so that the construction

```
for k,v in pairs(t) do body end
```

will iterate over all key–value pairs of table t.

See function next for the caveats of modifying the table during its traversal.

pcall (f, arg1, ···)

Calls function f with the given arguments in *protected mode*. This means that any error inside f is not propagated; instead, pcall catches the error and returns a status code. Its first result is the status code (a boolean), which is true if the call succeeds without errors. In such case, pcall also returns all results from the call, after this first result. In case of any error, pcall returns **false** plus the error message.

print (···)

Receives any number of arguments, and prints their values to stdout, using the tostring function to convert them to strings. print is not intended for formatted output, but only as a quick way to show a value, typically for debugging. For formatted output, use string.format.

rawequal (v1, v2)

Checks whether v1 is equal to v2, without invoking any metamethod. Returns a boolean.

rawget (table, index)

Gets the real value of table[index], without invoking any metamethod. table must be a table; index may be any value.

rawset (table, index, value)

Sets the real value of table[index] to value, without invoking any metamethod. table must be a table, index any value different from **nil**, and value any Lua value.

This function returns table.

select (index, ···)

If index is a number, returns all arguments after argument number index. Otherwise, index must be the string "#", and select returns the total number of extra arguments it received.

setfenv (f, table)

Sets the environment to be used by the given function. f can be a Lua function or a number that specifies the function at that stack level: Level 1 is the function calling setfenv. setfenv returns the given function.

As a special case, when f is 0 setfenv changes the environment of the running thread. In this case, setfenv returns no values.

setmetatable (table, metatable)

Sets the metatable for the given table. (You cannot change the metatable of other types from Lua, only from C.) If metatable is **nil**, removes the metatable of the given table. If the original metatable has a "__metatable" field, raises an error.

This function returns table.

tonumber (e [, base])

Tries to convert its argument to a number. If the argument is already a number or a string convertible to a number, then tonumber returns this number; otherwise, it returns **nil**.

An optional argument specifies the base to interpret the numeral. The base may be any integer between 2 and 36, inclusive. In bases above 10, the letter 'A' (in either upper or lower case) represents 10, 'B' represents 11, and so forth, with 'Z' representing 35. In base 10 (the default), the number may have a decimal part, as well as an optional exponent part (see §2.1). In other bases, only unsigned integers are accepted.

tostring (e)

Receives an argument of any type and converts it to a string in a reasonable format. For complete control of how numbers are converted, use string.format.

If the metatable of e has a "__tostring" field, then tostring calls the corresponding value with e as argument, and uses the result of the call as its result.

type (v)

Returns the type of its only argument, coded as a string. The possible results of this function are "nil" (a string, not the value **nil**), "number", "string", "boolean", "table", "function", "thread", and "userdata".

unpack (list [, i [, j]])

Returns the elements from the given table. This function is equivalent to

```
return list[i], list[i+1], ···, list[j]
```

except that the above code can be written only for a fixed number of elements. By default, i is 1 and j is the length of the list, as defined by the length operator (see §2.5.5).

_VERSION

A global variable (not a function) that holds a string containing the current interpreter version. The current contents of this variable is "Lua 5.1".

xpcall (f, err)

This function is similar to pcall, except that you can set a new error handler.

xpcall calls function f in protected mode, using err as the error handler. Any error inside f is not propagated; instead, xpcall catches the error, calls the err function with the original error object, and returns a status code. Its first result is the status code (a boolean), which is true if the call succeeds without errors. In this case, xpcall also returns all results from the call, after this first result. In case of any error, xpcall returns **false** plus the result from err.

5.2 Coroutine Manipulation

The operations related to coroutines comprise a sub-library of the basic library and come inside the table coroutine. See §2.11 for a general description of coroutines.

coroutine.create (f)

Creates a new coroutine, with body f. f must be a Lua function. Returns this new coroutine, an object with type "thread".

coroutine.resume (co [, val1, ···])

Starts or continues the execution of coroutine co. The first time you resume a coroutine, it starts running its body. The values val1, ··· are passed as the arguments to the body function. If the coroutine has yielded, resume restarts it; the values val1, ··· are passed as the results from the yield.

If the coroutine runs without any errors, resume returns **true** plus any values passed to yield (if the coroutine yields) or any values returned by the body function (if the coroutine terminates). If there is any error, resume returns **false** plus the error message.

coroutine.running ()

Returns the running coroutine, or **nil** when called by the main thread.

coroutine.status (co)

Returns the status of coroutine co, as a string: "running", if the coroutine is running (that is, it called status); "suspended", if the coroutine is suspended in a call to yield, or if it has not started running yet; "normal" if the coroutine is active but not running (that is, it has resumed another coroutine); and "dead" if the coroutine has finished its body function, or if it has stopped with an error.

coroutine.wrap (f)

Creates a new coroutine, with body f. f must be a Lua function. Returns a function that resumes the coroutine each time it is called. Any arguments passed to the function behave as the extra arguments to resume. Returns the same values returned by resume, except the first boolean. In case of error, propagates the error.

coroutine.yield (···)

Suspends the execution of the calling coroutine. The coroutine cannot be running a C function, a metamethod, or an iterator. Any arguments to yield are passed as extra results to resume.

5.3 Modules

The package library provides basic facilities for loading and building modules in Lua. It exports two of its functions directly in the global environment: require and module. Everything else is exported in a table package.

module (name [, ···])

Creates a module. If there is a table in package.loaded[name], this table is the module. Otherwise, if there is a global table t with the given name, this table is the module. Otherwise creates a new table t and sets it as the value of the global name and the value of package.loaded[name]. This function also initializes t._NAME with the given name, t._M with the module (t itself), and t._PACKAGE with the package name (the full module name minus last component; see below). Finally, module sets t as the new environment of the current function and the new value of package.loaded[name], so that require returns t.

If name is a compound name (that is, one with components separated by dots), module creates (or reuses, if they already exist) tables for each component. For instance, if name is a.b.c, then module stores the module table in field c of field b of global a.

This function may receive optional *options* after the module name, where each option is a function to be applied over the module.

require (modname)

Loads the given module. The function starts by looking into the package.loaded table to determine whether modname is already loaded. If it is, then require returns the value stored at package.loaded[modname]. Otherwise, it tries to find a *loader* for the module.

To find a loader, first require queries package.preload[modname]. If it has a value, this value (which should be a function) is the loader. Otherwise require searches for a Lua loader using the path stored in package.path. If that also fails, it searches for a C loader using the path stored in package.cpath. If that also fails, it tries an *all-in-one* loader (see below).

When loading a C library, require first uses a dynamic link facility to link the application with the library. Then it tries to find a C function inside this library to be used as the loader. The name of this C function is the string "luaopen_" concatenated with a copy of the module name where each dot is replaced by an underscore. Moreover, if the module name has a hyphen, its prefix up to (and including) the first hyphen is removed. For instance, if the module name is a.v1-b.c, the function name will be luaopen_b_c.

If require finds neither a Lua library nor a C library for a module, it calls the *all-in-one loader*. This loader searches the C path for a library for the root name of the given module. For instance, when requiring a.b.c, it will search for a C library for a. If found, it looks into it for an open function for the submodule; in our example, that would be luaopen_a_b_c. With this facility, a package can pack several C submodules into one single library, with each submodule keeping its original open function.

Once a loader is found, require calls the loader with a single argument, modname. If the loader returns any value, require assigns the returned value to package.loaded[modname]. If the loader returns no value and has not assigned any value to package.loaded[modname], then require assigns **true** to this entry. In any case, require returns the final value of package.loaded[modname].

If there is any error loading or running the module, or if it cannot find any loader for the module, then require signals an error.

package.cpath

The path used by require to search for a C loader.

Lua initializes the C path package.cpath in the same way it initializes the Lua path package.path, using the environment variable LUA_CPATH (plus another default path defined in luaconf.h).

package.loaded

A table used by require to control which modules are already loaded. When you require a module modname and package.loaded[modname] is not false, require simply returns the value stored there.

package.loadlib (libname, funcname)

Dynamically links the host program with the C library libname. Inside this library, looks for a function funcname and returns this function as a C function. (So, funcname must follow the protocol (see lua_CFunction on page 32)).

This is a low-level function. It completely bypasses the package and module system. Unlike require, it does not perform any path searching and does not automatically adds extensions. libname must be the complete file name of the C library, including if necessary a path and extension. funcname must be the exact name exported by the C library (which may depend on the C compiler and linker used).

This function is not supported by ANSI C. As such, it is only available on some platforms (Windows, Linux, Mac OS X, Solaris, BSD, plus other Unix systems that support the dlfcn standard).

package.path

The path used by require to search for a Lua loader.

At start-up, Lua initializes this variable with the value of the environment variable LUA_PATH or with a default path defined in luaconf.h, if the environment variable is not defined. Any "; ;" in the value of the environment variable is replaced by the default path.

A path is a sequence of *templates* separated by semicolons. For each template, require will change each interrogation mark in the template by filename, which is modname with each dot replaced by a "directory separator" (such as "/" in Unix); then it will try to load the resulting file name. So, for instance, if the Lua path is

```
"./?.lua;./?.lc;/usr/local/?/init.lua"
```

the search for a Lua loader for module foo will try to load the files ./foo.lua, ./foo.lc, and /usr/local/foo/init.lua, in that order.

package.preload

A table to store loaders for specific modules (see require on page 72).

package.seeall (module)

Sets a metatable for module with its __index field referring to the global environment, so that this module inherits values from the global environment. To be used as an option to function module.

5.4   String Manipulation

This library provides generic functions for string manipulation, such as finding and extracting substrings, and pattern matching. When indexing a string in Lua, the first character is at position 1 (not at 0, as in C). Indices are allowed to be negative and are interpreted as indexing backwards, from the end of the string. Thus, the last character is at position –1, and so on.

The string library provides all its functions inside the table `string`. It also sets a metatable for strings where the `__index` field points to the `string` table. Therefore, you can use the string functions in object-oriented style. For instance, `string.byte(s,i)` can be written as `s:byte(i)`.

string.byte (s [, i [, j]])

Returns the internal numerical codes of the characters `s[i]`, `s[i+1]`, ···, `s[j]`. The default value for `i` is 1; the default value for `j` is `i`.

Note that numerical codes are not necessarily portable across platforms.

string.char (···)

Receives zero or more integers. Returns a string with length equal to the number of arguments, in which each character has the internal numerical code equal to its corresponding argument.

Note that numerical codes are not necessarily portable across platforms.

string.dump (function)

Returns a string containing a binary representation of the given function, so that a later `loadstring` on this string returns a copy of the function. `function` must be a Lua function without upvalues.

string.find (s, pattern [, init [, plain]])

Looks for the first match of `pattern` in the string `s`. If it finds a match, then `find` returns the indices of `s` where this occurrence starts and ends; otherwise, it returns **nil**. A third, optional numerical argument `init` specifies where to start the search; its default value is 1 and may be negative. A value of **true** as a fourth, optional argument `plain` turns off the pattern matching facilities, so the function does a plain "find substring" operation, with no characters in `pattern` being considered "magic". Note that if `plain` is given, then `init` must be given as well.

If the pattern has captures, then in a successful match the captured values are also returned, after the two indices.

string.format (formatstring, ···)

Returns a formatted version of its variable number of arguments following the description given in its first argument (which must be a string). The format string follows the same rules as the `printf` family of standard C functions.

The only differences are that the options/modifiers *, l, L, n, p, and h are not supported and that there is an extra option, q. The q option formats a string in a form suitable to be safely read back by the Lua interpreter: the string is written between double quotes, and all double quotes, newlines, embedded zeros, and backslashes in the string are correctly escaped when written. For instance, the call

```
string.format('%q', 'a string with "quotes" and \n new line')
```

will produce the string:

```
"a string with \"quotes\" and \
 new line"
```

The options c, d, E, e, f, g, G, i, o, u, X, and x all expect a number as argument, whereas q and s expect a string.

This function does not accept string values containing embedded zeros.

string.gmatch (s, pattern)

Returns an iterator function that, each time it is called, returns the next captures from pattern over string s.

If pattern specifies no captures, then the whole match is produced in each call.

As an example, the following loop

```
s = "hello world from Lua"
for w in string.gmatch(s, "%a+") do
  print(w)
end
```

will iterate over all the words from string s, printing one per line. The next example collects all pairs key=value from the given string into a table:

```
t = {}
s = "from=world, to=Lua"
for k, v in string.gmatch(s, "(%w+)=(%w+)") do
  t[k] = v
end
```

string.gsub (s, pattern, repl [, n])

Returns a copy of s in which all occurrences of the pattern have been replaced by a replacement string specified by repl, which may be a string, a table, or a function. gsub also returns, as its second value, the total number of substitutions made.

If repl is a string, then its value is used for replacement. The character % works as an escape character: any sequence in repl of the form %n, with n between 1 and 9, stands for the value of the n-th captured substring (see below). The sequence %0 stands for the whole match. The sequence %% stands for a single %.

If repl is a table, then the table is queried for every match, using the first capture as the key; if the pattern specifies no captures, then the whole match is used as the key.

If repl is a function, then this function is called every time a match occurs, with all captured substrings passed as arguments, in order; if the pattern specifies no captures, then the whole match is passed as a sole argument.

If the value returned by the table query or by the function call is a string or a number, then it is used as the replacement string; otherwise, if it is **false** or **nil**, then there is no replacement (that is, the original match is kept in the string).

The optional last parameter n limits the maximum number of substitutions to occur. For instance, when n is 1 only the first occurrence of pattern is replaced.

Here are some examples:

```
x = string.gsub("hello world", "(%w+)", "%1 %1")
→ x="hello hello world world"

x = string.gsub("hello world", "%w+", "%0 %0", 1)
→ x="hello hello world"

x = string.gsub("hello world from Lua", "(%w+)%s*(%w+)", "%2 %1")
→ x="world hello Lua from"

x = string.gsub("home = $HOME, user = $USER", "%$(%w+)", os.getenv)
→ x="home = /home/roberto, user = roberto"

x = string.gsub("4+5 = $return 4+5$", "%$(.-)%$", function (s)
      return loadstring(s)()
    end)
→ x="4+5 = 9"

local t = {name="lua", version="5.1"}
x = string.gsub("$name%-$version.tar.gz", "%$(%w+)", t)
→ x="lua-5.1.tar.gz"
```

string.len (s)

Receives a string and returns its length. The empty string "" has length 0. Embedded zeros are counted, so "a\000bc\000" has length 5.

string.lower (s)

Receives a string and returns a copy of this string with all uppercase letters changed to lowercase. All other characters are left unchanged. The definition of what an uppercase letter is depends on the current locale.

string.match (s, pattern [, init])

Looks for the first *match* of pattern in the string s. If it finds one, then match returns the captures from the pattern; otherwise it returns **nil**. If pattern specifies no captures, then the whole match is returned. A third, optional numerical argument init specifies where to start the search; its default value is 1 and may be negative.

string.rep (s, n)

Returns a string that is the concatenation of n copies of the string s.

string.reverse (s)

Returns a string that is the string s reversed.

string.sub (s, i [, j])

Returns the substring of s that starts at i and continues until j; i and j may be negative. If j is absent, then it is assumed to be equal to –1 (which is the same as the string length). In particular, the call string.sub(s,1,j) returns a prefix of s with length j, and string.sub(s,-i) returns a suffix of s with length i.

string.upper (s)

Receives a string and returns a copy of this string with all lowercase letters changed to uppercase. All other characters are left unchanged. The definition of what a lowercase letter is depends on the current locale.

5.4.1 Patterns

Character Class: A *character class* is used to represent a set of characters. The following combinations are allowed in describing a character class:

x: (where *x* is not one of the *magic characters* ^$()%.[]*+-?) represents the character *x* itself.

.: (a dot) represents all characters.

%a: represents all letters.

%c: represents all control characters.

%d: represents all digits.

%l: represents all lowercase letters.

%p: represents all punctuation characters.

%s: represents all space characters.

%u: represents all uppercase letters.

%w: represents all alphanumeric characters.

%x: represents all hexadecimal digits.

%z: represents the character with representation 0.

%*x*: (where *x* is any non-alphanumeric character) represents the character *x*. This is the standard way to escape the magic characters. Any punctuation character (even the non magic) can be preceded by a '%' when used to represent itself in a pattern.

[*set*]: represents the class which is the union of all characters in *set*. A range of characters may be specified by separating the end characters of the range with a '-'. All classes %*x* described above may also be used as components in *set*. All other characters in *set* represent themselves. For example, [%w_] (or [_%w]) represents all alphanumeric characters plus the underscore, [0-7] represents the octal digits, and [0-7%l%-] represents the octal digits plus the lowercase letters plus the '-' character.

The interaction between ranges and classes is not defined. Therefore, patterns like [%a-z] or [a-%%] have no meaning.

[^*set*]: represents the complement of *set*, where *set* is interpreted as above.

For all classes represented by single letters (%a, %c, etc.), the corresponding uppercase letter represents the complement of the class. For instance, %S represents all non-space characters.

The definitions of letter, space, and other character groups depend on the current locale. In particular, the class [a-z] may not be equivalent to %l.

Pattern Item: A *pattern item* may be

- a single character class, which matches any single character in the class;

- a single character class followed by '*', which matches 0 or more repetitions of characters in the class. These repetition items will always match the longest possible sequence;

- a single character class followed by '+', which matches 1 or more repetitions of characters in the class. These repetition items will always match the longest possible sequence;

- a single character class followed by '-', which also matches 0 or more repetitions of characters in the class. Unlike '*', these repetition items will always match the *shortest* possible sequence;

- a single character class followed by '?', which matches 0 or 1 occurrence of a character in the class;

- %*n*, for *n* between 1 and 9; such item matches a substring equal to the *n*-th captured string (see below);

- %b*xy*, where *x* and *y* are two distinct characters; such item matches strings that start with *x*, end with *y*, and where the *x* and *y* are *balanced*. This means that, if one reads the string from left to right, counting +1 for an *x* and −1 for a *y*, the ending *y* is the first *y* where the count reaches 0. For instance, the item %b() matches expressions with balanced parentheses.

Pattern: A *pattern* is a sequence of pattern items. A '~' at the beginning of a pattern anchors the match at the beginning of the subject string. A '$' at the end of a pattern anchors the match at the end of the subject string. At other positions, '~' and '$' have no special meaning and represent themselves.

Captures: A pattern may contain sub-patterns enclosed in parentheses; they describe *captures*. When a match succeeds, the substrings of the subject string that match captures are stored (*captured*) for future use. Captures are numbered according to their left parentheses. For instance, in the pattern "(a*(.)%w(%s*))", the part of the string matching "a*(.)%w(%s*)" is stored as the first capture (and therefore has number 1); the character matching "." is captured with number 2, and the part matching "%s*" has number 3.

As a special case, the empty capture () captures the current string position (a number). For instance, if we apply the pattern "()aa()" on the string "flaaap", there will be two captures: 3 and 5.

A pattern cannot contain embedded zeros. Use %z instead.

5.5 Table Manipulation

This library provides generic functions for table manipulation. It provides all its functions inside the table table.

Most functions in the table library assume that the table represents an array or a list. For these functions, when we talk about the "length" of a table we mean the result of the length operator.

table.concat (table [, sep [, i [, j]]])

Returns table[i]..sep..table[i+1]···sep..table[j]. The default value for sep is the empty string, the default for i is 1, and the default for j is the length of the table. If i is greater than j, returns the empty string.

table.insert (table, [pos,] value)

Inserts element value at position pos in table, shifting up other elements to open space, if necessary. The default value for pos is n+1, where n is the length of the table (see §2.5.5), so that a call table.insert(t,x) inserts x at the end of table t.

table.maxn (table)

Returns the largest positive numerical index of the given table, or zero if the table has no positive numerical indices. (To do its job this function does a linear traversal of the whole table.)

table.remove (table [, pos])

Removes from table the element at position pos, shifting down other elements to close the space, if necessary. Returns the value of the removed element. The default value for pos is n, where n is the length of the table, so that a call table.remove(t) removes the last element of table t.

table.sort (table [, comp])

Sorts table elements in a given order, *in-place*, from table[1] to table[n], where n is the length of the table. If comp is given, then it must be a function that receives two table elements, and returns true when the first is less than the second (so that not comp(a[i+1],a[i]) will be true after the sort). If comp is not given, then the standard Lua operator < is used instead.

The sort algorithm is not stable; that is, elements considered equal by the given order may have their relative positions changed by the sort.

5.6 Mathematical Functions

This library is an interface to the standard C math library. It provides all its functions inside the table math.

math.abs (x)

Returns the absolute value of x.

math.acos (x)

Returns the arc cosine of x (in radians).

math.asin (x)

Returns the arc sine of x (in radians).

math.atan (x)

Returns the arc tangent of x (in radians).

math.atan2 (x, y)

Returns the arc tangent of x/y (in radians), but uses the signs of both parameters to find the quadrant of the result. (It also handles correctly the case of y being zero.)

math.ceil (x)

Returns the smallest integer larger than or equal to x.

math.cos (x)

Returns the cosine of x (assumed to be in radians).

math.cosh (x)
Returns the hyperbolic cosine of x.

math.deg (x)
Returns the angle x (given in radians) in degrees.

math.exp (x)
Returns the the value e^x.

math.floor (x)
Returns the largest integer smaller than or equal to x.

math.fmod (x, y)
Returns the remainder of the division of x by y.

math.frexp (x)
Returns m and e such that $x = m2^e$, e is an integer and the absolute value of m is in the range $[0.5, 1)$ (or zero when x is zero).

math.huge
The value HUGE_VAL, a value larger than or equal to any other numerical value.

math.ldexp (m, e)
Returns $m2^e$ (e should be an integer).

math.log (x)
Returns the natural logarithm of x.

math.log10 (x)
Returns the base-10 logarithm of x.

math.max (x, $\cdots$)
Returns the maximum value among its arguments.

math.min (x, $\cdots$)
Returns the minimum value among its arguments.

math.modf (x)
Returns two numbers, the integral part of x and the fractional part of x.

math.pi

The value of π.

math.pow (x, y)

Returns x^y. (You can also use the expression x^y to compute this value.)

math.rad (x)

Returns the angle x (given in degrees) in radians.

math.random ([m [, n]])

This function is an interface to the simple pseudo-random generator function rand provided by ANSI C. (No guarantees can be given for its statistical properties.)

When called without arguments, returns a pseudo-random real number in the range $[0,1)$. When called with a number m, math.random returns a pseudo-random integer in the range $[1,m]$. When called with two numbers m and n, math.random returns a pseudo-random integer in the range $[m,n]$.

math.randomseed (x)

Sets x as the "seed" for the pseudo-random generator: equal seeds produce equal sequences of numbers.

math.sin (x)

Returns the sine of x (assumed to be in radians).

math.sinh (x)

Returns the hyperbolic sine of x.

math.sqrt (x)

Returns the square root of x. (You can also use the expression x^0.5 to compute this value.)

math.tan (x)

Returns the tangent of x (assumed to be in radians).

math.tanh (x)

Returns the hyperbolic tangent of x.

5.7   Input and Output Facilities

The I/O library provides two different styles for file manipulation. The first one uses implicit file descriptors; that is, there are operations to set a default input file and a default output file, and all input/output operations are over these default files. The second style uses explicit file descriptors.

When using implicit file descriptors, all operations are supplied by table io. When using explicit file descriptors, the operation io.open returns a file descriptor and then all operations are supplied as methods of the file descriptor.

The table io also provides three predefined file descriptors with their usual meanings from C: io.stdin, io.stdout, and io.stderr.

Unless otherwise stated, all I/O functions return **nil** on failure (plus an error message as a second result) and some value different from **nil** on success.

io.close ([file])

Equivalent to file:close(). Without a file, closes the default output file.

io.flush ()

Equivalent to file:flush over the default output file.

io.input ([file])

When called with a file name, it opens the named file (in text mode), and sets its handle as the default input file. When called with a file handle, it simply sets this file handle as the default input file. When called without parameters, it returns the current default input file.

In case of errors this function raises the error, instead of returning an error code.

io.lines ([filename])

Opens the given file name in read mode and returns an iterator function that, each time it is called, returns a new line from the file. Therefore, the construction

```
for line in io.lines(filename) do body end
```

will iterate over all lines of the file. When the iterator function detects the end of file, it returns **nil** (to finish the loop) and automatically closes the file.

The call io.lines() (with no file name) is equivalent to io.input():lines(); that is, it iterates over the lines of the default input file. In this case it does not close the file when the loop ends.

io.open (filename [, mode])

This function opens a file, in the mode specified in the string mode. It returns a new file handle, or, in case of errors, **nil** plus an error message.

The mode string can be any of the following:

"r": read mode (the default);

"w": write mode;

"a": append mode;

"r+": update mode, all previous data is preserved;

"w+": update mode, all previous data is erased;

"a+": append update mode, previous data is preserved, writing is only allowed at the end of file.

The mode string may also have a 'b' at the end, which is needed in some systems to open the file in binary mode. This string is exactly what is used in the standard C function fopen.

io.output ([file])

Similar to io.input, but operates over the default output file.

io.popen (prog [, mode])

Starts program prog in a separated process and returns a file handle that you can use to read data from this program (if mode is "r", the default) or to write data to this program (if mode is "w").

This function is system dependent and is not available on all platforms.

io.read (···)

Equivalent to io.input():read.

io.tmpfile ()

Returns a handle for a temporary file. This file is opened in update mode and it is automatically removed when the program ends.

io.type (obj)

Checks whether obj is a valid file handle. Returns the string "file" if obj is an open file handle, "closed file" if obj is a closed file handle, or **nil** if obj is not a file handle.

io.write (···)

Equivalent to io.output():write.

file:close ()

Closes `file`. Note that files are automatically closed when their handles are garbage collected, but that takes an unpredictable amount of time to happen.

file:flush ()

Saves any written data to `file`.

file:lines ()

Returns an iterator function that, each time it is called, returns a new line from the file. Therefore, the construction

```
for line in file:lines() do body end
```

will iterate over all lines of the file. (Unlike `io.lines`, this function does not close the file when the loop ends.)

file:read (···)

Reads the file `file`, according to the given formats, which specify what to read. For each format, the function returns a string (or a number) with the characters read, or **nil** if it cannot read data with the specified format. When called without formats, it uses a default format that reads the entire next line (see below).

The available formats are

"*n": reads a number; this is the only format that returns a number instead of a string.

"*a": reads the whole file, starting at the current position. On end of file, it returns the empty string.

"*l": reads the next line (skipping the end of line), returning **nil** on end of file. This is the default format.

number: reads a string with up to this number of characters, returning **nil** on end of file. If number is zero, it reads nothing and returns an empty string, or **nil** on end of file.

file:seek ([whence] [, offset])

Sets and gets the file position, measured from the beginning of the file, to the position given by `offset` plus a base specified by the string `whence`, as follows:

"set": base is position 0 (beginning of the file);

"cur": base is current position;

"end": base is end of file;

In case of success, function seek returns the final file position, measured in bytes from the beginning of the file. If this function fails, it returns **nil**, plus a string describing the error.

The default value for whence is "cur", and for offset is 0. Therefore, the call file:seek() returns the current file position, without changing it; the call file:seek("set") sets the position to the beginning of the file (and returns 0); and the call file:seek("end") sets the position to the end of the file, and returns its size.

file:setvbuf (mode [, size])

Sets the buffering mode for an output file. There are three available modes:

"no": no buffering; the result of any output operation appears immediately.

"full": full buffering; output operation is performed only when the buffer is full (or when you explicitly flush the file (see io.flush on page 83)).

"line": line buffering; output is buffered until a newline is output or there is any input from some special files (such as a terminal device).

For the last two cases, sizes specifies the size of the buffer, in bytes. The default is an appropriate size.

file:write (···)

Writes the value of each of its arguments to the file. The arguments must be strings or numbers. To write other values, use tostring or string.format before write.

5.8 Operating System Facilities

This library is implemented through table os.

os.clock ()

Returns an approximation of the amount in seconds of CPU time used by the program.

os.date ([format [, time]])

Returns a string or a table containing date and time, formatted according to the given string format.

If the time argument is present, this is the time to be formatted (see the os.time function for a description of this value). Otherwise, date formats the current time.

If format starts with '!', then the date is formatted in Coordinated Universal Time. After this optional character, if format is the string "*t", then date returns a table with the following fields: year (four digits), month (1–12), day (1–31), hour (0–23), min (0–59), sec (0–61), wday (weekday, Sunday is 1), yday (day of the year), and isdst (daylight saving flag, a boolean).

If format is not "*t", then date returns the date as a string, formatted according to the same rules as the C function strftime.

When called without arguments, date returns a reasonable date and time representation that depends on the host system and on the current locale (that is, os.date() is equivalent to os.date("%c")).

os.difftime (t2, t1)

Returns the number of seconds from time t1 to time t2. In POSIX, Windows, and some other systems, this value is exactly t2−t1.

os.execute ([command])

This function is equivalent to the C function system. It passes command to be executed by an operating system shell. It returns a status code, which is system-dependent. If command is absent, then it returns nonzero if a shell is available and zero otherwise.

os.exit ([code])

Calls the C function exit, with an optional code, to terminate the host program. The default value for code is the success code.

os.getenv (varname)

Returns the value of the process environment variable varname, or **nil** if the variable is not defined.

os.remove (filename)

Deletes the file or directory with the given name. Directories must be empty to be removed. If this function fails, it returns **nil**, plus a string describing the error.

os.rename (oldname, newname)

Renames file or directory named oldname to newname. If this function fails, it returns **nil**, plus a string describing the error.

os.setlocale (locale [, category])

Sets the current locale of the program. locale is a string specifying a locale; category is an optional string describing which category to change: "all", "collate", "ctype", "monetary", "numeric", or "time"; the default category is "all". The function returns the name of the new locale, or **nil** if the request cannot be honored.

When called with **nil** as the first argument, this function only returns the name of the current locale for the given category.

os.time ([table])

Returns the current time when called without arguments, or a time representing the date and time specified by the given table. This table must have fields year, month, and day, and may have fields hour, min, sec, and isdst (for a description of these fields, see the os.date function).

The returned value is a number, whose meaning depends on your system. In POSIX, Windows, and some other systems, this number counts the number of seconds since some given start time (the "epoch"). In other systems, the meaning is not specified, and the number returned by time can be used only as an argument to date and difftime.

os.tmpname ()

Returns a string with a file name that can be used for a temporary file. The file must be explicitly opened before its use and explicitly removed when no longer needed.

5.9   The Debug Library

This library provides the functionality of the debug interface to Lua programs. You should exert care when using this library. The functions provided here should be used exclusively for debugging and similar tasks, such as profiling. Please resist the temptation to use them as a usual programming tool: they can be very slow. Moreover, several of its functions violate some assumptions about Lua code (e.g., that variables local to a function cannot be accessed from outside or that userdata metatables cannot be changed by Lua code) and therefore can compromise otherwise secure code.

All functions in this library are provided inside the debug table. All functions that operate over a thread have an optional first argument which is the thread to operate over. The default is always the current thread.

debug.debug ()

Enters an interactive mode with the user, running each string that the user enters. Using simple commands and other debug facilities, the user can inspect global and local variables, change their values, evaluate expressions, and so on. A line containing only the word cont finishes this function, so that the caller continues its execution.

Note that commands for debug.debug are not lexically nested within any function, and so have no direct access to local variables.

debug.getfenv (o)

Returns the environment of object o.

debug.gethook (`[thread]`)

Returns the current hook settings of the thread, as three values: the current hook function, the current hook mask, and the current hook count (as set by the `debug.sethook` function).

debug.getinfo (`[thread,] function [, what]`)

Returns a table with information about a function. You can give the function directly, or you can give a number as the value of `function`, which means the function running at level `function` of the call stack of the given thread: level 0 is the current function (`getinfo` itself); level 1 is the function that called `getinfo`; and so on. If `function` is a number larger than the number of active functions, then `getinfo` returns **nil**.

The returned table may contain all the fields returned by `lua_getinfo`, with the string `what` describing which fields to fill in. The default for `what` is to get all information available, except the table of valid lines. If present, the option 'f' adds a field named `func` with the function itself. If present, the option 'L' adds a field named `activelines` with the table of valid lines.

For instance, the expression `debug.getinfo(1,"n").name` returns a name of the current function, if a reasonable name can be found, and the expression `debug.getinfo(print)` returns a table with all available information about the `print` function.

debug.getlocal (`[thread,] level, local`)

This function returns the name and the value of the local variable with index `local` of the function at level `level` of the stack. (The first parameter or local variable has index 1, and so on, until the last active local variable.) The function returns **nil** if there is no local variable with the given index, and raises an error when called with a `level` out of range. (You can call `debug.getinfo` to check whether the level is valid.)

Variable names starting with '(' (open parentheses) represent internal variables (loop control variables, temporaries, and C function locals).

debug.getmetatable (`object`)

Returns the metatable of the given `object` or **nil** if it does not have a metatable.

debug.getregistry ()

Returns the registry table (see §3.5).

debug.getupvalue (`func, up`)

This function returns the name and the value of the upvalue with index up of the function `func`. The function returns **nil** if there is no upvalue with the given index.

debug.setfenv (`object, table`)

Sets the environment of the given `object` to the given `table`. Returns `object`.

debug.sethook (`[thread,] hook, mask [, count]`)

Sets the given function as a hook. The string `mask` and the number `count` describe when the hook will be called. The string mask may have the following characters, with the given meaning:

"`c`": The hook is called every time Lua calls a function;

"`r`": The hook is called every time Lua returns from a function;

"`l`": The hook is called every time Lua enters a new line of code.

With a `count` different from zero, the hook is called after every `count` instructions.

When called without arguments, `debug.sethook` turns off the hook.

When the hook is called, its first parameter is a string describing the event that has triggered its call: "`call`", "`return`" (or "`tail return`"), "`line`", and "`count`". For line events, the hook also gets the new line number as its second parameter. Inside a hook, you can call `getinfo` with level 2 to get more information about the running function (level 0 is the `getinfo` function, and level 1 is the hook function), unless the event is "`tail return`". In this case, Lua is only simulating the return, and a call to `getinfo` will return invalid data.

debug.setlocal (`[thread,] level, local, value`)

This function assigns the value `value` to the local variable with index `local` of the function at level `level` of the stack. The function returns **nil** if there is no local variable with the given index, and raises an error when called with a `level` out of range. (You can call `getinfo` to check whether the level is valid.) Otherwise, it returns the name of the local variable.

debug.setmetatable (`object, table`)

Sets the metatable for the given `object` to the given `table` (which can be **nil**).

debug.setupvalue (`func, up, value`)

This function assigns the value `value` to the upvalue with index `up` of the function `func`. The function returns **nil** if there is no upvalue with the given index. Otherwise, it returns the name of the upvalue.

debug.traceback (`[thread,] [message] [, level]`)

Returns a string with a traceback of the call stack. An optional `message` string is appended at the beginning of the traceback. An optional `level` number tells at which level to start the traceback (default is 1, the function calling `traceback`).

6 Lua Stand-alone

Although Lua has been designed as an extension language, to be embedded in a host C program, it is also frequently used as a stand-alone language. An interpreter for Lua as a stand-alone language, called simply `lua`, is provided with the standard distribution. The stand-alone interpreter includes all standard libraries, including the debug library. Its usage is:

```
lua [options] [script [args]]
```

The options are:

-`e`*stat*: executes string *stat*;

-`l`*mod*: "requires" *mod*;

-`i`: enters interactive mode after running *script*;

-`v`: prints version information;

`--`: stops handling options;

`-`: executes `stdin` as a file and stops handling options.

After handling its options, `lua` runs the given *script*, passing to it the given *args* as string arguments. When called without arguments, `lua` behaves as `lua -v -i` when the standard input (`stdin`) is a terminal, and as `lua -` otherwise.

Before running any argument, the interpreter checks for an environment variable `LUA_INIT`. If its format is `@`*filename*, then `lua` executes the file. Otherwise, `lua` executes the string itself.

All options are handled in order, except `-i`. For instance, an invocation like

```
$ lua -e'a=1' -e 'print(a)' script.lua
```

will first set a to 1, then print the value of a (which is '1'), and finally run the file `script.lua` with no arguments. (Here $ is the shell prompt. Your prompt may be different.)

Before starting to run the script, `lua` collects all arguments in the command line in a global table called `arg`. The script name is stored at index 0, the first argument after the script name goes to index 1, and so on. Any arguments before the script name (that is, the interpreter name plus the options) go to negative indices. For instance, in the call

```
$ lua -la b.lua t1 t2
```

the interpreter first runs the file `a.lua`, then creates a table

```
arg = { [-2] = "lua", [-1] = "-la",
        [0] = "b.lua",
        [1] = "t1", [2] = "t2" }
```

and finally runs the file b.lua. The script is called with arg[1], arg[2], ⋯ as arguments; it can also access these arguments with the vararg expression '...'.

In interactive mode, if you write an incomplete statement, the interpreter waits for its completion by issuing a different prompt.

If the global variable _PROMPT contains a string, then its value is used as the prompt. Similarly, if the global variable _PROMPT2 contains a string, its value is used as the secondary prompt (issued during incomplete statements). Therefore, both prompts can be changed directly on the command line. For instance,

```
$ lua -e"_PROMPT='myprompt> '" -i
```

(the outer pair of quotes is for the shell, the inner pair is for Lua), or in any Lua programs by assigning to _PROMPT. Note the use of -i to enter interactive mode; otherwise, the program would just end silently right after the assignment to _PROMPT.

To allow the use of Lua as a script interpreter in Unix systems, the stand-alone interpreter skips the first line of a chunk if it starts with #. Therefore, Lua scripts can be made into executable programs by using chmod +x and the #! form, as in

```
#!/usr/local/bin/lua
```

(Of course, the location of the Lua interpreter may be different in your machine. If lua is in your PATH, then

```
#!/usr/bin/env lua
```

is a more portable solution.)

7   Incompatibilities with the Previous Version

Here we list the incompatibilities that you may found when moving a program from Lua 5.0 to Lua 5.1. You can avoid most of the incompatibilities compiling Lua with appropriate options (see file `luaconf.h`). However, all these compatibility options will be removed in the next version of Lua.

7.1   Changes in the Language

- The vararg system changed from the pseudo-argument `arg` with a table with the extra arguments to the vararg expression. (See compile-time option `LUA_COMPAT_VARARG` in `luaconf.h`.)

- There was a subtle change in the scope of the implicit variables of the **for** statement and for the **repeat** statement.

- The long string/long comment syntax (`[[`*string*`]]`) does not allow nesting. You can use the new syntax (`[=[`*string*`]=]`) in these cases. (See compile-time option `LUA_COMPAT_LSTR` in `luaconf.h`.)

7.2   Changes in the Libraries

- Function `string.gfind` was renamed `string.gmatch`. (See compile-time option `LUA_COMPAT_GFIND` in `luaconf.h`.)

- When `string.gsub` is called with a function as its third argument, whenever this function returns **nil** or **false** the replacement string is the whole match, instead of the empty string.

- Function `table.setn` was deprecated. Function `table.getn` corresponds to the new length operator (#); use the operator instead of the function. (See compile-time option `LUA_COMPAT_GETN` in `luaconf.h`.)

- Function `loadlib` was renamed `package.loadlib`. (See compile-time option `LUA_COMPAT_LOADLIB` in `luaconf.h`.)

- Function `math.mod` was renamed `math.fmod`. (See compile-time option `LUA_COMPAT_MOD` in `luaconf.h`.)

- Functions `table.foreach` and `table.foreachi` are deprecated. You can use a for loop with `pairs` or `ipairs` instead.

- There were substantial changes in function `require` due to the new module system. However, the new behavior is mostly compatible with the old, but `require` gets the path from `package.path` instead of from `LUA_PATH`.

- Function `collectgarbage` has different arguments. Function `gcinfo` is deprecated; use `collectgarbage("count")` instead.

7.3 Changes in the API

- The `luaopen_*` functions (to open libraries) cannot be called directly, like a regular C function. They must be called through Lua, like a Lua function.

- Function `lua_open` was replaced by `lua_newstate` to allow the user to set a memory-allocation function. You can use `luaL_newstate` from the standard library to create a state with a standard allocation function (based on `realloc`).

- Functions `luaL_getn` and `luaL_setn` (from the auxiliary library) are deprecated. Use `lua_objlen` instead of `luaL_getn` and nothing instead of `luaL_setn`.

- Function `luaL_openlib` was replaced by `luaL_register`.

- Function `luaL_checkudata` now throws an error when the given value is not a userdata of the expected type. (In Lua 5.0 it returned NULL.)

8 The Complete Syntax of Lua

Here is the complete syntax of Lua in extended BNF. (It does not describe operator precedences.)

$$
\begin{aligned}
\mathit{chunk} \;\;&\rightarrow\;\; \{\mathit{stat}\;[\text{`;'}]\}\,[\,\mathit{laststat}\;[\text{`;'}]\,] \\
\mathit{block} \;\;&\rightarrow\;\; \mathit{chunk} \\
\mathit{stat} \;\;&\rightarrow\;\; \mathit{varlist1}\;\text{`='}\;\mathit{explist1} \\
&\;\;|\;\; \mathit{functioncall} \\
&\;\;|\;\; \textbf{do}\;\mathit{block}\;\textbf{end} \\
&\;\;|\;\; \textbf{while}\;\mathit{exp}\;\textbf{do}\;\mathit{block}\;\textbf{end} \\
&\;\;|\;\; \textbf{repeat}\;\mathit{block}\;\textbf{until}\;\mathit{exp} \\
&\;\;|\;\; \textbf{if}\;\mathit{exp}\;\textbf{then}\;\mathit{block}\;\{\textbf{elseif}\;\mathit{exp}\;\textbf{then}\;\mathit{block}\}\,[\,\textbf{else}\;\mathit{block}\,]\;\textbf{end} \\
&\;\;|\;\; \textbf{for}\;\text{Name}\;\text{`='}\;\mathit{exp}\;\text{`,'}\;\mathit{exp}\,[\,\text{`,'}\;\mathit{exp}\,]\;\textbf{do}\;\mathit{block}\;\textbf{end} \\
&\;\;|\;\; \textbf{for}\;\mathit{namelist}\;\textbf{in}\;\mathit{explist1}\;\textbf{do}\;\mathit{block}\;\textbf{end} \\
&\;\;|\;\; \textbf{function}\;\mathit{funcname}\;\mathit{funcbody} \\
&\;\;|\;\; \textbf{local function}\;\text{Name}\;\mathit{funcbody} \\
&\;\;|\;\; \textbf{local}\;\mathit{namelist}\,[\,\text{`='}\;\mathit{explist1}\,] \\
\mathit{laststat} \;\;&\rightarrow\;\; \textbf{return}\;[\,\mathit{explist1}\,]\;|\;\textbf{break} \\
\mathit{funcname} \;\;&\rightarrow\;\; \text{Name}\;\{\text{`.'}\;\text{Name}\}\,[\,\text{`:'}\;\text{Name}\,] \\
\mathit{varlist1} \;\;&\rightarrow\;\; \mathit{var}\;\{\text{`,'}\;\mathit{var}\} \\
\mathit{var} \;\;&\rightarrow\;\; \text{Name}\;|\;\mathit{prefixexp}\;\text{`['}\;\mathit{exp}\;\text{`]'}\;|\;\mathit{prefixexp}\;\text{`.'}\;\text{Name} \\
\mathit{namelist} \;\;&\rightarrow\;\; \text{Name}\;\{\text{`,'}\;\text{Name}\} \\
\mathit{explist1} \;\;&\rightarrow\;\; \{\mathit{exp}\;\text{`,'}\}\,\mathit{exp} \\
\mathit{exp} \;\;&\rightarrow\;\; \textbf{nil}\;|\;\textbf{false}\;|\;\textbf{true}\;|\;\text{Number}\;|\;\text{String}\;|\;\text{`...'}\;|\;\mathit{function} \\
&\;\;|\;\; \mathit{prefixexp}\;|\;\mathit{tableconstructor}\;|\;\mathit{exp}\;\mathit{binop}\;\mathit{exp}\;|\;\mathit{unop}\;\mathit{exp} \\
\mathit{prefixexp} \;\;&\rightarrow\;\; \mathit{var}\;|\;\mathit{functioncall}\;|\;\text{`('}\;\mathit{exp}\;\text{`)'} \\
\mathit{functioncall} \;\;&\rightarrow\;\; \mathit{prefixexp}\;\mathit{args}\;|\;\mathit{prefixexp}\;\text{`:'}\;\text{Name}\;\mathit{args} \\
\mathit{args} \;\;&\rightarrow\;\; \text{`('}\,[\,\mathit{explist1}\,]\,\text{`)'}\;|\;\mathit{tableconstructor}\;|\;\text{String} \\
\mathit{function} \;\;&\rightarrow\;\; \textbf{function}\;\mathit{funcbody} \\
\mathit{funcbody} \;\;&\rightarrow\;\; \text{`('}\,[\,\mathit{parlist1}\,]\,\text{`)'}\;\mathit{block}\;\textbf{end} \\
\mathit{parlist1} \;\;&\rightarrow\;\; \mathit{namelist}\,[\,\text{`,'}\;\text{`...'}\,]\;|\;\text{`...'} \\
\mathit{tableconstructor} \;\;&\rightarrow\;\; \text{`\{'}\,[\,\mathit{fieldlist}\,]\,\text{`\}'} \\
\mathit{fieldlist} \;\;&\rightarrow\;\; \mathit{field}\;\{\mathit{fieldsep}\;\mathit{field}\}\,[\,\mathit{fieldsep}\,] \\
\mathit{field} \;\;&\rightarrow\;\; \text{`['}\;\mathit{exp}\;\text{`]'}\;\text{`='}\;\mathit{exp}\;|\;\text{Name}\;\text{`='}\;\mathit{exp}\;|\;\mathit{exp} \\
\mathit{fieldsep} \;\;&\rightarrow\;\; \text{`,'}\;|\;\text{`;'} \\
\mathit{binop} \;\;&\rightarrow\;\; \text{`+'}\;|\;\text{`-'}\;|\;\text{`*'}\;|\;\text{`/'}\;|\;\text{`\textasciicircum'}\;|\;\text{`\%'}\;|\;\text{`..'} \\
&\;\;|\;\; \text{`<'}\;|\;\text{`<='}\;|\;\text{`>'}\;|\;\text{`>='}\;|\;\text{`=='}\;|\;\text{`\textasciitilde='} \\
&\;\;|\;\; \textbf{and}\;|\;\textbf{or} \\
\mathit{unop} \;\;&\rightarrow\;\; \text{`-'}\;|\;\textbf{not}\;|\;\text{`\#'}
\end{aligned}
$$

Index